To Hope,
A little bit of
I hope

Kenny xx

WE
GAVE A
DAM

The epic race to build
the Thames Barrier

WE GAVE A DAM

The epic race to build the Thames Barrier

RORY O'GRADY

We Gave a Dam: The epic race to build the Thames Barrier

Published by The Conrad Press Ltd. in the United Kingdom 2024

Tel: +44(0)1227 472 874

www.theconradpress.com

info@theconradpress.com

ISBN 978-1-916966-45-1

Typesetting by: www.bookstyle.co.uk

Cover design by Terrybannon.com with images: Main Photo: Copyright: Petr Svec | Dreamstime Inset Back Cover: Copyright: I Wei Huang | Dreamstime

The Conrad Press logo was designed by Maria Priestley.

Printed and bound in Great Britain by Clays Ltd, Elcograf S.p.A.

By the same author

Stonecutters Bridge, Gateway to Hong Kong's Port
Bonham Media, Hong Kong, 2010

The Passionate Imperialists
The Conrad Press, United Kingdom, 2018

The Flight of The Arctic Fox
The Conrad Press, United Kingdom, 2021

In memory of Edgar McGuiness, and dedicated to Ray Horner, Project Manager of the GLC, and to all those who designed, fabricated, managed, and worked on the Thames Barrier.

Contents

LIST OF PLATES

PART 1

The Consultant - Rendel Palmer and Tritton

PART 2

The Gate Contractor - DCBC

Final Works

AERIAL PHOTOGRAPHS by Aero Industrial Photographic Services, Wantage Berkshire, Others by Tom Samson FBIIP, Handford Photography, and Costain Group Photographic Unit, unless otherwise stated.

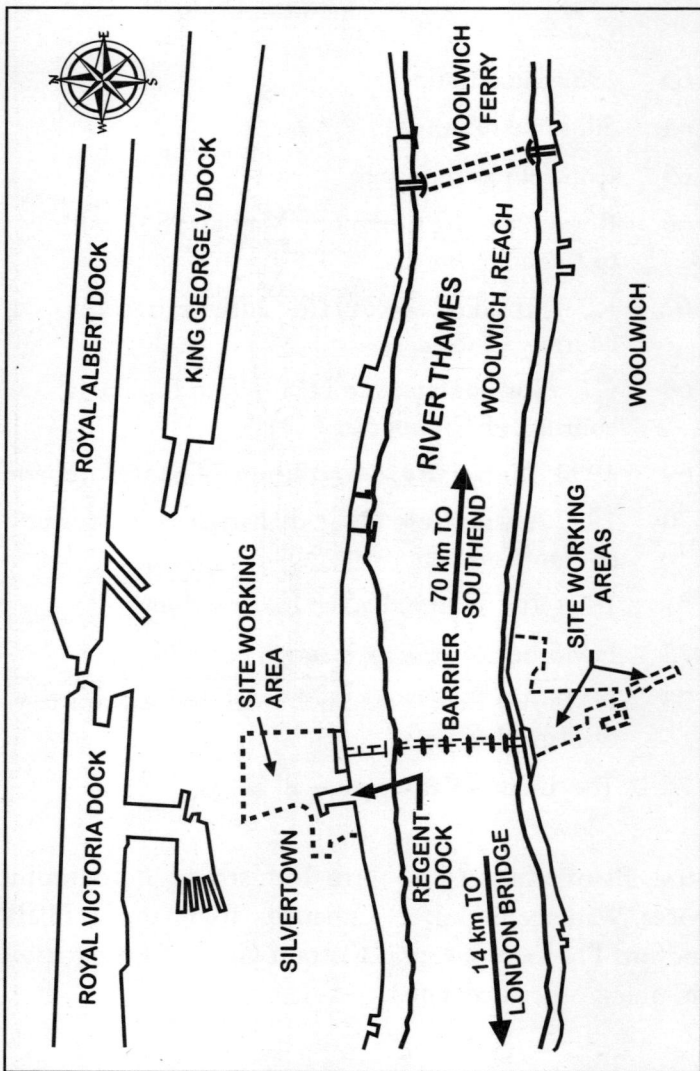

Fig 1. Location of The Thames Barrier

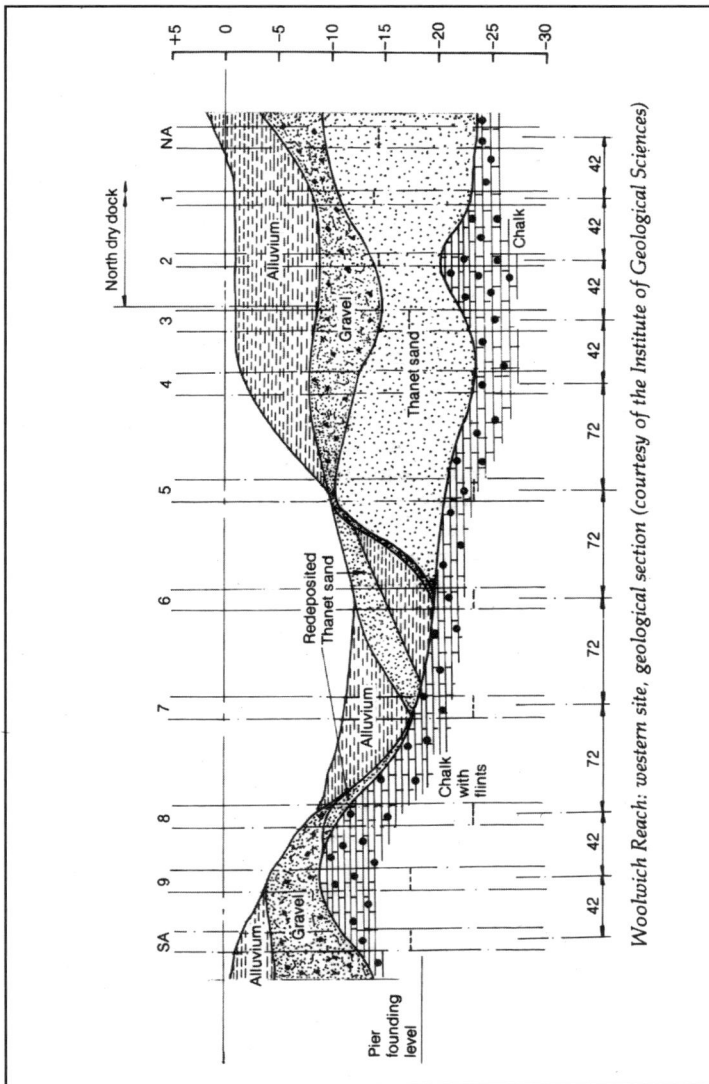

Woolwich Reach: western site, geological section (courtesy of the Institute of Geological Sciences)

Fig 2. Geological section at the barrier

PREFACE

The Thames Barrier is now considered one of the seven wonders of the modern world. It is a magnificent piece of British engineering, and has received numerous well-deserved accolades.

This was not always the case. It had taken thirty years to get the barrier completed since the last major floods in 1953. Why had it taken so long?

On February 1 1953, there was widespread damage, and over 300 people drowned when a tidal surge rolled down the east coast of England. It swept up the Thames Estuary and broke through many of the existing Thames flood defences. It got close to spilling over the embankments in central London. This would have led to flooding of the London underground stations near to the river and submerging the low-lying streets with a possible huge loss of life. Electricity, gas and water supplies would have been seriously disrupted, which would have taken many months to reconnect. It could have easily crashed the economy, and would have been a catastrophe.

Various designs had been put forward after World War II, but in 1953 Britain was still recovering from the war and the subsequent recession. Money for any kind of significant investment was in very short supply, and there were many politicians who had higher spending priorities.

At that time, London Docks was vital to the economy, and it was essential that trade was not disrupted. The Port of London

Authority (PLA) controlled every aspect of shipping in the Thames and any barrier would need their approval.

This significantly delayed decisions on the location, type and cost of a barrier. In that respect, it was fortunate that the final design was not decided until the arrival of the container terminal at Tilbury, and the subsequent rapid decline of London Docks in the 1970s.

A key figure who helped solve the impasse with the PLA was Professor Sir Hermann Bondi, who produced an enlightened Report in 1967, which helped the PLA to reconsider their strict conditions. Woolwich Reach became acceptable as a site and enabled detailed design to press ahead. By 1972, the design and estimated costs were able to be presented to Parliament.

The politicians were in no mood to sanction investing large amounts of money in major civil engineering works, despite the fact it had been proven that repairing flood damage would be many times the cost of building a barrier. Inflation was rampant, prices were spiralling and the Conservative government was on its last legs.

The presentation of the Private Bill to Parliament needed to be skilled and convincing. It was headed by Ray Horner from the GLC, backed up by Peter Cox, the senior partner from the designers, and representatives from the Kent and Essex River Boards. They did a fine job and convinced the politicians of the requirement and urgency of the barrier. The Bill received Royal Assent in August 1972, and the tender documents for the civil engineering contract were issued in early 1973.

Contractors were naturally reticent to tender, due to the complexity and economic uncertainties at the time, and only three consortium tenders were returned. After hard negotiations, an agreement was reached and the contract was awarded to the consortium of Costain Civil Engineering, Tarmac Construction, and HBM BV, and the contract was signed in July 1974.

The work commenced on site in January 1975, and during the following eight years, a series of major problems were thrown at the contractors. These varied from unforeseen engineering problems, numerous industrial actions, increasing tidal surges and extremes of weather, through a backdrop of difficult political and economic times. They were overcome by tenacity, ingenuity and the close cooperation of all parties involved, and the constant reminder that time was not on their side.

Despite the severe delays, the Thames Barrier was operational by 1982 and was opened with great celebration by HM Queen Elizabeth II on May 8 1984.

I worked for five years with the civils contractor as a young civil engineer on this unique project between 1975 and 1980. This book tells the story of the building of the Thames Barrier, from the memories of many of those that had the fortune to work on it during its construction.

It tells of the trials, tribulations and triumphs during those very difficult and challenging years, and the feeling of immense pride for what was achieved. It is the story of the men and women that worked on the site, and also a tribute to the many thousands of people in design offices, factories and workshops, not only across the British Isles, but in Holland, Austria and the USA, who made valuable contributions to this truly iconic structure.

1

THE INTERVIEW

In October 1975, I was travelling out of London on a crowded, noisy, uncomfortable commuter train, attempting to read the evening paper, when I spotted an advert in the Job Vacancies page that immediately caught my attention. An open evening was to be held in a hotel at Bexley in south-east London to recruit staff for a joint venture that had recently been awarded a new project called the Thames Barrier.

I was a twenty-five-year-old civil engineer coming to the end of a job with a major contractor building the southern section of the M11 motorway. It had been an interesting project, starting with a complex intersection involving high viaducts flying over the busy North Circular Road and finishing on the edge of Epping Forest, in the delights of rural Essex.

We had used an old pub called The Charlie Brown as our site office. It was full of character and a well-known meeting place for villains from the East End of London. The early seventies was a time of high inflation, soaring prices, and crippling industrial action by coal miners and railway workers. During the winter of 1974, the power was restricted to three days a week, resulting in us huddling around candles in the office after sunset, wearing many layers of clothing trying to keep warm, as we sorted out problems and planned the schedule of the next day's work. It was a scene worthy of a Charles Dickens story. Oil prices had doubled and any contractors who had bid with fixed prices were doomed, resulting in many going bankrupt. Hard times indeed.

Seeing a major new engineering project starting in these difficult times, with guaranteed work for a minimum of two years, was very welcome, and I quickly noted down the details of the venue.

Two weeks later, I arrived in the early evening at the Black Prince Hotel in Bexley, close to the A2 dual carriageway, a constantly choked artery from Kent into London. The hotel was a large, mock-Tudor style establishment that had started life as a pub in the 1930s, and had become a popular music venue by the 1970s. It had large function rooms that were ideal for company events. I joined a long line of prospective hopefuls in front of a cluster of tables, at which were seated managers from the joint venture interviewing potential recruits.

I was introduced to David Hoare, the deputy project manager of the contractor CTH Joint Venture (CTHJV), comprising Costain Civil Engineering, Tarmac Construction, and a large Dutch marine company called Hollandsche Beton Maatschappij (HBM), which was part of a bigger Dutch conglomerate called HBG.

David was still in his early thirties but because of his rapid hair loss, along with his crumpled grey suit, he looked a lot older. He was from Wolverhampton and spoke with the unsettling tones of a strong, Midlands accent. He came across as an intelligent, no-nonsense character with a nervous, powerful energy and an infectious passion for the barrier, which grew as the interview progressed.

After a brief introduction and a few questions about my previous engineering experience, he asked me if I knew anything about the Thames Barrier. I acknowledged I had only read a little about the history of why it was needed, and had only seen artists' impressions of the finished structure. However, I knew little about how it was going to be built. For the next twenty minutes David explained the sequence of construction, with drawings, pamphlets and sketches, showing what was going to unfold over the next five years. The size of the project was awe-inspiring; everything was on such an immense scale.

To build the permanent works, vast, cathedral-like coffer-dams needed to be constructed across the River Thames. These are temporary steel boxes made from interlocking sheet piles with internal struts, which, after dewatering would allow the permanent structure to be built in the dry.

The excavations would be up to twenty-five metres below the river bed level, with concrete plugs consisting of over six thousand cubic metres of underwater concrete needed for the foundations of each of the nine piers. Abutments would be at either side of the river giving a total width of 560 metres. To get to the cofferdams, large, temporary access jetties would be built out across the Thames, to transport workers and materials, and a large variety of heavy plant. A massive, temporary dry dock would be built on the north side, where the concrete sills weighing up to 10,000 tonnes would be precast and eventually floated out and sunk between the piers. Each concrete pier would be the equivalent of building a twelve-storey office block in the middle of the Thames.

The massive steel gates between the concrete piers would be fabricated by a contractor in Darlington and transported by barge down the east coast and up the Thames. They would weigh up to 1500 tonnes, and require two of the largest floating cranes in Europe to lift them into place.

I had never worked on a project of this scale, and from what David was saying, I quickly realised I was not alone. He understood this, and was looking for engineers who would not be daunted by the size, and would rise to the challenges of inevitable problems that would be presented on such a unique structure. I was exhilarated at the thought of being involved. A few days later I was offered the position as a site engineer, and started at the CTHJV site office the following month.

On returning home that evening, I was eager to find out more of the history of why the Thames Barrier became necessary to build, and how its design evolved.

2

HISTORY

When the Romans first arrived in Britain in 55BC led by Julius Caesar, the Thames was a much narrower river, and it was not tidal at London Bridge. By 1099 the river was wider, deeper and faster flowing, and the Anglo-Saxon Chronicle recorded a record height in early November which '...*caused much harm in the area.*' This was only sixty-four years after King Canute, the ruler of a North Sea empire covering England, Denmark and Norway, had sat on his throne at the river's edge at Westminster giving a demonstration of his humility to his courtiers. He commanded the tide to stop as the water surged around his feet. When it continued to rise, he leapt back and admonished his courtiers for thinking that the power of kings was capable of turning the tide.

Another flood is recorded in 1236 when '...*The river was reported as overflowing, and in the great Palace of Westminster, men did row with wherries in the middle of the hall....*' On December 7 1663, Samuel Pepys recorded in his diary that '...*At Whitehall I hear and find there was the greatest tide that ever was remembered in England to have been in this river. All Whitehall having been drowned, there was great discourse...*'

Further surge tides were recorded in 1791, 1834, 1852, 1874 and 1875, but January 7 1928 was the last time central London was flooded. The surge peaked in the early hours. Fourteen people drowned in their basements near the river and thousands were made homeless. Water poured in over the top of the Thames Embankment and part of the Chelsea embankment collapsed, with the flooding affecting areas as far downriver as Greenwich and Woolwich.

THE GREAT FLOOD 1953

On February 1 1953, the surge level at London Bridge was 250mm higher than the 1928 level. The sea defences were overwhelmed down the east coast, where 300 people drowned, and 30,000 had to leave their homes. Canvey Island was inundated and 58 lives were lost, 41 died at Felixstowe and 37 perished at Jaywick, near Clacton. Deaths at sea totaled 224, including a roll on/roll off ferry, the *MV Princess Victoria* operating between Stranraer in Scotland and Larne in Northern Ireland. She sank in the North Channel on the previous night with the loss of 135 lives. In Holland the devastation was far worse where over 3000 drowned or died from exposure.

Most of London had been spared, but the magnitude of the damage caused by the surge was a real wake-up call. The Waverley Committee was set up by Parliament in April 1953 chaired by Sir John Anderson to examine the dangers, and to make recommendations. It was obvious that the North Sea storms causing the surges were getting stronger, but the reasons were not understood.

The Committee published a report in 1954 recommending further research into the nature of surge tides, and that a new storm surge barrier across the Thames should be built, which would allow free passage to tides and shipping. Long Reach, twenty miles downriver from London Bridge, between Purfleet and Tilbury, was suggested as a suitable site. At this time London docks were one of the biggest in the world and essential for the country's trade. They employed over 30,000 workers, making the Port of London Authority (PLA) a very powerful body. The PLA was intransigent in the choice of location for a barrier, and with the widths of the shipping lanes. This dramatically increased the width of the barrier required, along with the estimated costs.

A NEW IMPETUS

For the next ten years, testing was carried out at the Hydraulic Research Station (HRS), Wallingford, in Oxfordshire, and proposals and counter proposals were submitted for Long Reach. At the same time major changes were being proposed for local government, which inevitably slowed decisions.

From 1889, the London administrative body for London was the London County Council (LCC). After the devastation of World War II, it was evident that the LCC was too small to cope with the enormous demands being placed on it, and in 1960, a Royal Commission recommended a major restructuring of local government. It wanted to abolish all existing London local authorities except the City of London Corporation, and form a Greater London Council (GLC), along with thirty-two new, lower-tier London boroughs. The London Act Bill was introduced in 1963, and the first elections were held in 1964. After a one-year transition, the LCC was abolished, and on April 1 1965 was replaced by the GLC.

Everything could start moving again, and the GLC was invited to take over the development of the Thames Barrier and the downriver flood protection works, under the responsibility of the Director of Public Health Engineering.

In 1966, the Government's Principal Scientific Advisor, Sir (later Lord) Solly Zuckerman, was consulted to bring in a fresh view-point. He recommended that a high-ranking scientist of Nobel Prize calibre should investigate and produce a report with his recommendations. The person he had in mind looked a strange choice on paper, but was perfect.

Professor Sir Hermann Bondi was an astronomer, a Professor of Mathematics and had been involved in Space, Defence and Power committees, and came to the barrier debate with no preconceived ideas or allegiances. He was the breath of fresh air that was required, and after reviewing the existing proposals and visiting the different sites, he quickly came to the conclusion that the cost of building a barrier would be far less than the cost of dealing with a flood. He also concluded that the probability of greater surges in the near future was high, and urgent decisions were needed.

An important innovation had occurred since the Waverly Report. The age of the container had arrived, and the first new terminal was being built at Tilbury docks. For the first time in its long history, river traffic through the London docks was dropping significantly, and was a signal of what was to be repeated across all the major ports of Britain over the following decades. This gave the PLA more flexibility for the choice of width of the navigational openings required during construction of the barrier, and improved the chances of a better economic solution. The Bondi report did not recommend a site, but did say the Woolwich Reach area should also be considered as an option, where the width of the river was much narrower.

The Bondi Report was submitted on November 21 1967 to the Ministry of Housing, who invited the GLC to undertake an urgent investigation into comparing the construction of a movable barrier at Woolwich Reach and Crayfordness. Two experienced maritime consultants, Rendel, Palmer and Tritton (RPT), and Sir Bruce White and Partners, who had been working on the earlier schemes, were reappointed to work on the two shortlisted locations.

By the summer of 1969, it was possible to narrow down the range of possibilities. Shortly after this time, the closure of Surrey Docks was announced, with West India Docks close behind. Up to this time, the main spans of all the alternatives was dictated by the PLA as 450ft. (137 metres), to cater for vessels moving to these docks. This width could be reviewed, and Woolwich Reach would become a far more economical option. The span could now be dictated by the span of Tower Bridge. This was only 200ft, (61 metres) but vessels up to 20,000 tonnes had been passing through it for eighty years with few mishaps. This was considered a powerful argument to put forward to the PLA.

A Policy Committee was formed, chaired by Lord Kennett, with a Steering Committee overseeing another nine sub-committees coordinating the many parties who would become involved. This was when Ray Horner, a senior manager with the GLC, became part of the team.

I only met Ray Horner once, on the barrier at a reunion in 1992, shortly after he retired. He was in his seventies then, of a congenial disposition, conservatively dressed, always seen with a jacket and tie, and sporting a neat moustache. He was studious, knowledgeable, and tenacious - the perfect person to drive a committee. My understanding was that he joined the GLC shortly after it was formed, in 1965, and was quickly appointed as Project Manager of the Barrier Steering Committee, with the job of driving forward all the sub-committees to get the barrier built.

These committees covered a wide range of interested parties and subjects, including the Navigation Working Party, the Oceanographical and Meteorological Working Party, the Civil Engineering Working Party, the Pollution and Siltation Working Party, the Groundwater Effects Group, and the Amenities Working Party. Continuous regular meetings were held over many years, and Ray was admired for his stamina and patience, commuting back and forth every day from his family home in Stokes Poges, near Slough, always keeping the momentum going.

He was immensely proud of his contribution, and is rightly known as '*The Father of the Barrier.*'

WOOLWICH REACH DESIGN

Six different designs were considered, with the First Report of Studies published in 1969. During the meeting of the Policy Committee on September 29 1969, a danger warning was issued along the east coast of the country predicting surge levels at the Humber and Lincolnshire higher than those of 1953. Considerable flooding was experienced in Hull and the devastation it caused focused the minds of the committee significantly. Three designs were rejected. Everyone quickly agreed that the widths of the main navigation spans for a barrier to be built at Woolwich Reach should be 200ft. (61m). It was clear this scheme should now be developed at Woolwich Reach, and the exact site needed to be finalised urgently.

A shortlist of sites was looked at along Woolwich Reach, and the most suitable was opposite a large Tate & Lyle sugar beet factory. However, the cost of compensation to the company would have been way too high. A second site near the old Woolwich Dockyard was objected to by Greenwich Council, due to planning being well-advanced for a large housing development. Finally, a western site became available on both sides, at Charlton on the south, and Silvertown on the north, and detailed design could now proceed.

The GLC and Greenwich Council were against drop gates for the barrier on aesthetic grounds. An alternative was a drum gate, but this was costly, requiring far deeper excavations. It was at this time that one of RPT's senior technicians, Charles 'Charlie' Draper, had a 'eureka' moment in his house in Horsham on a cold winter's day just before Christmas.

He was looking at the simple valve mechanism on a gas pipe, and realised the principle could be considered for rotating a rising sector gate, but on an altogether larger scale. He could not wait to get to the office the next day to present his idea to the design team. They were intrigued, and after discussing it could see no reason why the idea couldn't be developed further.

The engineers looked at a method to rotate the gates from the resting position on the river bed, through ninety degrees to the closed position, and finally up to a maintenance position, using gate arms powered by hydraulic cylinders. The gate could be housed in a concrete sill positioned on the river bed, when it was in the resting position. Not only did this design avoid the deep excavations required for the drum gate, but closing was a positive action by powerful hydraulic machinery.

Draper's relatively simple solution would be easy to operate, it looked good, and it would provide large cost savings that would please all parties.

Reginald Charles Draper was born in Edmonton, north London in 1932, and had younger brother Frank. The two boys were evacuated at the beginning of World War Two in 1939 and attended school in Halstead, Essex. He joined Rendel, Palmer and Tritton as a draughtsman when he was seventeen years old, and apart from a short spell of National Service, he spent his entire working life with RPT in their Head Office, first in Victoria Street, London, and later Southwark Street. He worked alongside the engineers, and enjoyed participating in discussions to find innovative solutions to awkward problems, particularly in the field of moving structures such as bascule bridges and dock gates.

His finest hour was coming up with the simple idea of a gas valve being considered as the mechanism for the Thames Barrier gates, which the engineers then developed and proved could work. This story captured the imagination of the press, and he enjoyed his new found fame.

On September 19 1979, Charlie, as he liked to be called, was invited to the 60th anniversary of the Institute of Patentees and Inventors, at the Royal Society in the City of London Rooms. There was an impressive and sophisticated exhibition of thirty of the members' inventions, including a model of the Thames Barrier gates. The occasion was reported in *The Sunday Telegraph* a few days later by the columnist Mandrake, who said, '*It was sad to report that within this British Institution, the inventor is not as eccentric as they might be, for a more sober-suited, immaculately groomed gallery you could not find. Far from being wild-eyed dishevelled things, they were quietly articulate, and had invented things like the Thames Flood Barrier and the Automatic Chip Dispensing Machine!*'

Charles married Diane Bunker in 1954, who sadly died of cancer, and he remarried in 1983 to Betty Flood, who was the RPT office manager. He was delighted to be able to visit the barrier in 1982 after it became operational, and I was very lucky to find a photo of that day of him standing on the south side, holding a cross section of a gas valve, with the piers stretching across the river. The expression on his face says everything.

He was a handsome and popular man with an ever-present cheerful disposition, greatly admired and who gained much respect from the staff who knew him. He was awarded the MBE before he died of cancer the following year aged 51, and was also awarded the Freedom of the City of London for his contribution to the barrier.

The final design was completed with four main navigation spans of 200ft (61 metres) using rising sector gates, and two further 100ft (31.5 metres) navigation spans using smaller rising sector gates. A further four 100ft spans were provided to allow the free flow of the tide through the structure, and fitted with simpler falling radial gates. Control of all these gates were from a control tower located on the south side.

By 1970, preliminary site investigations had started at Woolwich, initially with seven boreholes, followed by another seventy-three over 1972/73. Hydraulic model testing was carried out at the Hydraulic Research Station at Wallingford, and various model tests on the gates and sills were prepared at Imperial College, London.

To complete the final design and prepare the contract plan necessary for the construction of the work, the GLC needed to get approval from Parliament. The quickest way was to promote a Private Bill. It was presented in the autumn of 1971, and a small number of objections were lodged, which were overcome after further discussions with those concerned. The hearing of evidence took two weeks, with Ray Horner representing the GLC, the Kent and Essex river boards represented by their Chief Engineers, Jim Taylor and Ted Snell, and technical assistance provided by Peter Cox, senior partner of RPT. Everyone was given a fair hearing and the Bill passed the Committee stage with only minor amendments.

After passing through and getting approval from the House of Lords, the Bill received Royal Assent in August 1972.

THE DESIGNERS

Rendel Palmer and Tritton were appointed to complete the working drawings for the barrier, and to supervise construction on site. Sir Bruce White and Partners produced further designs for the flood prevention works downriver of the barrier.

RPT were well-established and highly respected consultants, founded by James Meadows Rendel in London in 1838, who became the 6th President of the Institution of Civil Engineers in 1853. He was famous for the design of a vast new dock in Grimsby completed in 1843. His son, Sir Alexander Rendel (1829 - 1938), expanded the consultancy into India with Frederick Palmer and Sir Seymour Tritton, designing major new bridges and marine works for the East India Company.

They set up their office in Victoria Street, Westminster, along with many other notable Victorian consultants who wanted to be within walking distance of the decision makers for the expanding British Empire. The company continued growing in the twentieth-century gaining an enviable reputation in docks, railways and bridges. In the 1960s, many consultants moved out of London, and in the mid-sixties, RPT moved across the river to new offices at 61, Southwark Street.

Peter Cox was the RPT partner chosen to see the Thames Barrier through to completion in 1972. He had extensive experience in marine and dock works around the world, and been involved with the development of the barrier design over many years. An intelligent, quiet man, who hid a very dramatic past, he had a great calming effect when discussions became heated. He had risen up through the ranks by his own special abilities.

Peter Arthur Cox was born in London in 1922 and went to school at Westcliffe High School in Essex. He left school at sixteen and in 1940 attended the City and Guilds College in London and studied for a BSc (Eng.) in Civil Engineering which, despite the war raging, he attained in 1942.

At the age of twenty, he joined the Royal Engineers and was commissioned a year later into the 51st (Antrim) Parachute Regiment. He was wounded by a mine in January 1945, and took part at the crossing of the Rhine (Operation Varsity) in March when his glider was the only one to arrive at the correct position at the bridges over the River Essel. He and a small party of sappers engaged in heavy fighting before the infantry captured the bridge, which the sappers successfully destroyed. They moved to another bridge which was under fire, and he had to crawl out on his stomach carrying one explosive charge at a time. This bridge was also destroyed before a counter-attack reached it. Peter was commended and mentioned in dispatches for his exploits. He continued in the Territorial Army after the war, and reached the rank of Colonel in 1981.

In 1947 he was demobbed from the Army, and joined the consulting engineers, Lewis and Duvivier in London. He built up his design experience over the next five years and qualified as a chartered civil engineer. From 1952 to 1954 he joined RPT for the first time, and followed by experience with Peter Lind & Co Limited and Sir Bruce White and Partners, who were working with RPT on the early barrier proposals.

He rejoined RPT as a resident engineer for a marine project in Iran, before returning to the UK for further work on port and marine works in the UK, Ireland, South America, Ethiopia, Qatar and Nigeria. The barrier was given parliamentary approval and for the next fourteen years, he was the Partner responsible for the completion of the project. He was totally dedicated, and in 1984 was presented to the Queen at the opening ceremony. In 1980 he was elected President of the Institution of Civil Engineers (ICE), in the footsteps of the founder of RPT, and became a Fellow of the Royal Academy of Engineering.

He was the last senior partner in Rendel Palmer and Tritton before they merged with High Point, to become High Point-Rendel in 1985. Peter continued his work with the ICE and had a leading role in an infrastructure planning group. The Government didn't think it was necessary, (probably because they hadn't thought of it), but the planning group became the concept for the National Infrastructure Commission, which was eventually set up in 2015. Engineers of Peter's calibre never really retire, and he died still working in 2018 aged 96.

In 1973 the pressure now fell on RPT to complete the thousands of drawings required for the project, with a large number required by the following year, when the tender would be issued. RPT had vast experience in marine works and docks, but needed to bring in more senior engineers with dam experience. RPT's Project Engineer for the barrier, George Carr, had worked with EPDC, the design company of Balfour Beatty, one of the major UK contractors. He remembered that Alan Mitchell, a very experienced senior engineer had ideal experience on large dams. They approached him, discussed the project, and quickly knew they had found the Chief Design Engineer to lead the civil works on the Thames Barrier.

Alan Ogston Mitchell was born in Aberdeen in 1933, and spent his childhood with his parents and elder brother and sister in 'The Granite City'. At sixteen Alan knew he wanted to go to university, but was still considering his options of what to study. A relative, also a civil engineer, suggested he should consider civil engineering. Engineers were in great demand after the war to spearhead recovery of the country, so plenty of jobs were available, and he would have the opportunity to leave a legacy. This caught Alan's imagination, and in 1951 he went to Aberdeen University to study for a degree in Civil Engineering. He graduated in 1954 and started work with Sir William Halcrow and Partners, a well-respected Scottish consultants, originally founded by Thomas Meik in 1875 in Edinburgh.

They had started with bridges, ports and railways in Scotland, including the Invergordan naval base at Scapa Flow in the Orkneys. This expanded into tunnels in London, and with the design of the Mulberry harbours which had been used on D-Day in 1944. In the 1950s there was a large expansion in the building of hydro-electric schemes in Scotland, Wales and northern England, and when Alan joined Halcrow in 1954, he started work on the Glenmoriston hydro-electric project in Scotland, which incorporated three dams and two power stations. He mainly supervised work on the Dundreggan underground power station and associated tunnels.

In 1956 he was called up for his national service and continued to gain civil engineering experience with a commission in the RAF airfield construction branch, with 18 months in Libya and Jordan undertaking the maintenance and expansion works in military airports. In 1958 he rejoined Halcrow and Partners working on coal-fired power stations and some early nuclear power stations. This gave him the design experience to enable him to become chartered, and became a Member of the Institution of Civil Engineers.

He left Halcrow in 1962, and in 1963 decided to widen his experience with a contractor. He applied for a planning post with Balfour Beatty, and at the interview learned that their design department (EPDC) had just been appointed with a Dutch firm to design and supervise the Kainji hydro-electric project in Nigeria. As a result, he accepted an offer in that department.

At that time, many African countries were gaining their independence from their former colonial powers. Money was becoming available from the World Bank to help these fledgling countries develop their infrastructure, and Kainji Dam was such a project. It was a massive scheme with a 72m high concrete intake dam and spillway totalling 7.2 kilometres long, positioned on the southern end of Kainji Lake reservoir, the largest artificial lake in Nigeria.

Alan soon found himself in charge of the design of the power stations and the administration building, set at the foot of the intake dam. He liaised with the World Bank representative on initial concepts, and with the manufacturers of the turbines, generators, cranes, control gates, and the Dutch architect for the superstructure. The design was carried out in London, with Alan visiting the site at regular intervals, experiencing the challenges of construction in Africa.

At this time, a particularly bitter civil war was raging in the south-east of Nigeria between 1967 and 1970, when Biafra was fighting to be a secessionist state. The war left 100,000 military casualties, and nearly two million Biafran civilians died of starvation. Despite all the setbacks the hostilities caused, this major project was completed successfully in 1968.

Alan had gained all this experience by the age of 40, and was about to be presented with his greatest challenge, working on the Thames Barrier.

After he had accepted the RPT offer of Chief Design Engineer for the civil works in 1973, Alan was given a large office in Southwark Street, close to the RPT Head Office which would be solely dedicated to the barrier. Here he quickly built a team of up to seventy staff to deliver thousands of working drawings to site.

A similar team was working on the gates and the mechanical and electrical works under the Chief Design Engineer for the mechanical works, Stuart Pratt, with whom Alan would work very closely. He would be unable to complete any of the machinery rooms until many of the critical components needed had been decided.

The RPT civil team liaised with the GLC architect's department who were designing the shell roofs for the piers and the onshore building works. RPT understood the concepts of the shell roof, but had to find ways the shells could be built with the least interruption to contractors working elsewhere on site. After lengthy discussions it was decided that the shells should be prefabricated offsite in sections, with vertical joints between them to be completed on site.

This hectic design schedule continued during the three-day working week, due to national industrial action. As a result, it was necessary to increase the office hours from 09:00 to 20:00.

Before the tender documents for the gates were issued, the RPT gates design team liaised with leading steel fabricators to get their views on the gate design, and likely methods they would use for the fabrication. The first consideration was whether the curved skin plate of the gates should be made from plates running transversely or longitudinally.

From the fabrication point of view, they were advised to have a longitudinal plate arrangement. The welding of the D-shaped gates should be carried out with the curved face upwards, which would be formed on a shaped stillage. The gates are hollow, but they are heavily braced inside with diaphragms and cross-members, easier to weld in this position. This was also the best way for transportation and erection on site. These discussions proved highly beneficial to the final design. The gates could be fabricated using well-established techniques, and were of enormous benefit later on.

In 1973, the GLC issued the tender documents, and the

initial demolition of a factory building on site at Eastmoor Street, Charlton began, allowing the opening up of large areas that would be required for the small army of contractors and consultants who would shortly be arriving.

3

1973 – 1975

1973
TENDERS ISSUED

When the civils contract was put out to tender in the winter of 1973, there was an understandable reticence by contractors to bid on a fixed price. In 1973, the UK was going through exceptional economic and political upheaval. The price of oil had rocketed, inflation was at 24%, and there was considerable industrial unrest - the miners had been striking, a three-day week had been introduced by the government and there were 1.25 million people out of work. The Conservative government was crumbling, and an election was imminent. It was a time of anxiety and great unknowns and the GLC was nervous to embark on a project of this size and complexity in a turbulent London docklands, where much of the labour would be sourced.

It was also not surprising that the interest from contractors was muted. The GLC could find only five contractors showing any interest, and just three of those consortia submitted tenders. After months of negotiations, during which all the bidders submitted heavily qualified costs, the detailed discussions came down to one consortium. Lengthy discussions continued night after night and the negotiators were exhausted.

The GLC finally agreed to include special conditions written into the Thames Barrier contract to give some reassurances to the contractor exposed to such high financial risks.

An important departure from the standard Conditions of Contract was that the civils works contractor would only be responsible for the cost of industrial disputes affecting the whole of the labour force for a total of twenty-one days for each year. It was also agreed that at the end of the first two years, the contract rates would be reviewed, and that the engineer, (RPT) would have the power to grant an extension of time for delays due to national shortages of materials, and disruption caused by government regulations in connection with fuel, power and other matters. Special consideration was also made for the exceptionally high inflation at that time.

1974
CONTRACTS SIGNED

After further discussions to obtain approval from the government, the Public Health Engineering Director of the GLC awarded the civils contract to CTH Joint Venture (CTHJV) consisting of Costain Civil Engineering (lead contractor with 36%), Tarmac Construction (32%) and Hollandsche Beton Maatschappij BV (32%), for £38.1m. It was signed in July 1974.

The contracts for the steel gates and the operating machinery were awarded to Davy-Loewy/Cleveland Bridge Consortium (DCBC) and did not have these clauses, as their contracts were more conventional, with less risk, and the work being carried out in factories in the north of England. However, the contracts did include clauses covering reimbursement for the contactor if inflation exceeded 25%.

In 1973, further contracts were let for the trunnions (the shaft support structures), diesel generators, switch-gear and transformers, control panels, mechanical and electrical services, onshore works, and lifts, navigation lights, dredging and assorted civil works.

All these contracts involved many individual companies and thousands of people all round the UK. The GLC Steering Committee led by Ray Horner worked flat out to build up momentum in the project.

1975
THE START OF CONSTRUCTION

In view of the size and complexity of the project, the CTHJV consortium was allowed six months to assemble plant, order materials, and find staff. The agreed start on site was in January 1975. This allowed initial dredging of the Thames to proceed with a separate contractor, requiring around a million cubic metres of material to be removed for a diversion channel to the north of the central pier, so enabling shipping to navigate through during construction. Unfortunately this led to the first fatality on the site when a lighterman fell from one of the spoil barges and was drowned.

CTHJV established offices both on the north and south sides, and prepared the quays and landing jetties on both sides. On the north side, the preparations started for the construction of the dry dock, and on the south side, piling for the access jetties started to push out across the Thames. It was hoped that the southern half of the barrier would be complete by summer 1977, when the river traffic would be diverted, but that turned out to be a far too optimistic deadline.

This was the situation when I arrived on site on a cold, misty November morning in 1975, when I reported to the CTHJV offices in Eastmoor Street, Charlton. This run-down area of south-east London had deteriorated rapidly since the 1960s, with many businesses and shops from Woolwich to Greenwich closed and derelict, and the skyline dominated by slabs of grey, depressing tower blocks.

There had been a history of shipbuilding along this stretch of the Thames going back over 500 years. Ships, constructed in both wood and steel, had been built and repaired here since it was founded by Henry VIII in 1513. Numerous small companies supplied specialist goods and services to London Docks, employing thousands of people, many of whom lived locally. The arrival of the first container terminal at Tilbury in 1967 heralded the dock closures that led to large numbers of unskilled workers being made redundant. The barrier was seen as a welcome sign of new opportunities in business and in jobs.

The CTHJV site office was a large, old, five-storey factory originally used for turbine testing by General Electric in the 1950s, and ideal for the many activities that the joint venture would undertake. It had been acquired by the GLC and cleared out, ready for the contractor. The ground floor had been converted into spacious welding, carpentry and plant shops, each with their own manager and team, plus the radio centre, safety and first aid offices.

The administration department was on the first floor led by the very capable Gwenda Brennan. Her office manager, the unflappable Brenda Harrop, had a post room and a team of twenty typists and clerks operating the clattering, ageing type-writers, consuming forests of paper, everything being issued a minimum in triplicate to the many companies involved.

On the second floor was the design department led by Chief Engineer Bob Napthine, who had been heavily involved in the tender. Bob was a highly experienced engineering manager who had worked with Costain since 1970.

Robert Napthine was born in the Rhondda Valley in 1935. This area in Glamorgan, South Wales, was famous first for coal, then the male voice choirs, the chapels, socialism, and a fervent love of rugby. In 1612 there were two mines recorded in the valley, and by 1893 there were seventy-five, extending seventy miles from Pontypool to St Brides, and covered 1,000 square miles. As a boy, in bed at night, he could hear the trains rattling up to the mines, and later when he played cricket for the local team, he would watch the weary miners coming off shift, tired, and covered in coal dust. It was a life he did not desire.

During World War II, Bob stayed in the Rhondda, continuing his education until he was eighteen. He was a good scholar, and in 1953 he won a place at Leeds University to study for a degree in Civil Engineering. He enjoyed his time at Leeds, and joined the University Air Squadron, where he learnt to fly Chipmunks.

He graduated in 1957, and was immediately called

up for National Service and chose to join the Royal Air Force (RAF). He continued flying, and learned to fly the Vampire jet, a turbojet fighter, the successor to the Gloster Meteor and the first single-engine turbojet fighter introduced into the RAF in 1946. When he finished his National Service, he returned to his career in civil engineering, but always had a love for flying.

In 1958 Bob joined British Rail Western Region as a graduate apprentice, as it had a very good training scheme. It covered all aspects of the diverse infrastructure of railway engineering, including bridges, tunnels, stations and operational buildings, over the western region. One interesting project was the replacement of Chepstow Railway Bridge on the Great Western Railway over the River Wye. It had been designed by Isambard Kingdom Brunel and opened in 1852. It was a tubular suspension bridge spanning 309 feet (91 metres) across the river, and considered one of his finest achievements. By 1960, some of the deck girders were showing some distortion and the whole deck had to be replaced. The original cast-iron column supports are still in use.

After a few years, Bob felt he needed to expand his design experience, and left British Rail to join a small consultants, Buck and Partners, in London. They were undertaking work in London and Kent, and Bob's projects included several bridges on the M2 motorway and the hovercraft terminal at Pegwell Bay, near Ramsgate. This experience was particularly useful. The geology at the barrier and terminal was similar and test drilling would be carried out at Ramsgate. After working in the design office, he was seconded to Higgs and Hill, a major building contractor specialising in tall tower blocks in London. With all this varied experience, he took the examination and qualified as a chartered civil engineer.

In 1963, he joined Rendel, Palmer and Tritton for three years in the London office to work on their design of Pembroke Power Station. This was a 2000MW oil-fired station with four 500MW turbo alternators. It was built in the mid-sixties and opened in 1968.

By 1970, Bob was ready for another change and moved to Costain International to work in the tender office in London, little knowing he would soon be meeting RPT again on the Thames Barrier.

The successful tender submissions with Costain included, the first tunnel under the harbour in Hong Kong, and the massive Dubai Dry dock in the United Arab Emirates. Costain had been working in Dubai for some years, and in 1971 helped develop the early planning for a project that many thought would never happen. It was the largest and only dry dock facility in the Persian Gulf, and Costain formed a joint venture with Taylor Woodrow to start construction in 1978, which was completed five years later. Spread over 200 acres, it covered four docks. The dock walls were constructed from massive caissons, built on land, and sunk into the sea. It required hundreds of engineers, most coming from the UK. Many Costain engineers returned to work in London with perfect experience for the barrier.

In 1973, the Thames Barrier tender was issued by

RPT, and Bob was seconded to work with a small team from Costain, Tarmac and HBM, based in offices in London and Holland. It was a very tight schedule. During that period of high inflation, it was very difficult to get sensible prices from suppliers, especially with such large quantities of materials involved. The steel for the temporary works took up nearly 50% of the total cost of the contract, and this was all based on a provisional design. Much reliance was put on the skill of the temporary works designers working in London and Holland getting their figures right. Much to their credit, when the final steel quantities were calculated, they were extremely close to the estimate in the tender.

As soon as CTHJV were informed they had won the contract in the summer of 1974, Bob was appointed Chief Engineer and sent to the site office in Charlton to set up the design office. He was still only thirty-nine years old.

He spent a year getting the team together. The designers needed to hit the ground running, and to commence the temporary works designs straight away. Much needed to be submitted and approved by RPT, and Bob rapidly established a good working relationship with the senior RPT and GLC managers based on site.

Costain had other ideas for him. After one year on site, he was promoted to Chief Engineering Manager of the Costain International Tenders office in London, as well as being asked by the new Project Manager, John Grice, to keep a watchful eye on the barrier design office. In 1977 he became a Fellow of the Institution of Civil

Engineers (FICE).

I worked with Bob in the London Office in 1980 for a few years. It was very busy with an excellent group of engineers and many successful tenders in Hong Kong, Nigeria, and the Middle East. In 1983 it looked pretty certain that the Channel Tunnel was going to be built, and Costain wanted to be involved. Bob was once again brought in to work on the planning for the tender, this time as part of an Anglo-French consortium Transmarche Link (TML), consisting of five UK companies and six French, making the bid a lot more complicated. TML were announced the winners by Eurotunnel in 1988, and Bob became totally immersed in yet another iconic project, based in the London and Folkestone offices for the next six years. It opened to much praise in 1994.

He returned to Head Office when the Channel Tunnel opened, and retired for a well-deserved rest in 1997. It had been an amazing career. He is still going strong in 2024, having a quieter life with his wife Ann in Kent.

When Bob left the barrier in 1976, Jan Van Ijken took over, with the sartorially elegant Don Langdown as Chief Engineering Manager.

The design department also included planners, the method statements team, and a large and talented crew of tempo-rary-works designers, including Amar Bhogal, who went on to become Chief Executive of the Institution of Civil Engineers. Tony Deane was a gifted designer, a Cambridge graduate who had come from Tarmac, and was joined by Stuart Marchand, and

Drick Vernon, with Hans Belksma from HBM. These design engineers were backed up by an equal number of essential skilled draughtsmen. HBM also had their own Dutch designers in an adjacent office working on the marine works led by Jan Van Ijken.

They would have to deliver the extensive, temporary structures designs, including the cofferdams, the working platforms and access jetties, all of which would have to get approval from RPT. These structures accounted for over half the cost of the project, and would require over 7000 drawings, so the pressure was on from the start to produce such a volume of submissions, including calculations. Bear in mind that in those days, everything was hand drawn, and slide rules were still being used. This was the pre-microcomputer age, but six new Hewlett Packard hand-held calculators were one of the first purchases for the design office.

Graham Storey and Peter Blaseby were the first two planners to arrive on site, and were soon joined by Phil Edwards, Gerry Munck, and a young student called Richard Bayfield.

Most planners used a simple arrow diagram system which could be done by hand, but with the number of construction activities involved in the building of the barrier, Costain were keen to develop their computer system using the latest Precedence Programme, which was still in its nursery days. The computers that did exist were very basic and large in 1975, using punch-card systems which were cumbersome and laborious, and so the data needed to be transferred to the head office computer every evening, and run overnight.

Inevitably the new computer systems were plagued with problems, and on site we didn't have time to wait for them to be fixed. It was quicker to break down the activities into simple, hand-written arrow diagrams, and get the planners to draw all the links in. The process was a whole universe away from the design power of today's computers.

On the upper floors of the site office were meeting rooms, administration, and senior management offices, including that of David Hoare, the senior Tarmac manager.

The Project Manager, David Derbyshire, had the office with the best view. He was thirty-eight years old, and a smart, ambitious, hard-working modern manager. He was also a ruthless squash player, as I soon found out when I joined the newly formed squash ladder, which became the perfect release for a frustrating day at work.

The view from his window looked out across the river to the north side in Silvertown, and over the adjacent car park to the RPT offices, led by George Davies the Engineer's Representative. They had been appointed to carry out the site supervision for the client, to see their design to completion. They would check our work on site, as well as inspect the permanent works being manufactured in workshops around the UK. As you can imagine, the connecting path between our offices would be well-worn by the end of the project.

George Davies was a hardened Welshman from the old school of consultants. They considered themselves Gods of the profession believing that lowly contractors should know their place, and be constantly watched for trying to cut corners and submitting inflated claims. George took an immediate dislike to David Derbyshire, who he considered far too young and smart for his own good to be a project manager of such a prestigious job, despite being well-educated and having solid management experience.

George was born in Wales in the 1920s and served in the Fleet Air Arm during World War II when he was barely twenty years old. He was awarded the Distinguished Service Cross for bravery, for helping defend Malta during their heroic siege. The island was bombed for 156 consecutive day and nights, and many British pilots died. George rarely talked about this time, and few office staff were aware of it. After the war he returned to Wales and studied for a degree in Civil Engineering at Cardiff University.

For five years he worked for a variety of contractors gaining site experience. In 1956, he joined RPT, first working on several power stations, including Aberthaw in Wales and Eggborough, in North Yorkshire, before going to Cyprus to work on an extension to Limassol Harbour.

In 1974, when he was is mid-fifties, he was appointed as the engineer's representative at the Thames Barrier site. It was a wide and challenging remit. He was responsible for steering through the often conflicting requirements of the many contractors on site, plus dealing with the GLC, the PLA and the MAFF. In addition, there was constant reporting and liaison with the RPT Head Office in London. Peter Cox, the senior partner, took a close interest, and once a month the chief design engineer, Alan Mitchell, came for a site visit to discuss any current problems there might be with any drawings that were causing delays.

In 1976, the contract review was undertaken with CTHJV, and the client used RPT to lead on a lot of the discussions. They were hard negotiations, and included an insistence to change some of the CTHJV senior managers. This is when John Grice was appointed, much to George Davies' delight. This developed into a far better relationship, and despite the occasional inevitable disagreements, it was a good and positive move for the contract.

George remained on site until the opening of the barrier and in 1983 he was awarded the MBE in the New Year's Honours List for services to his work on the barrier. He is quoted as saying, *'It makes me feel proud, particularly for all the people who have done the work. I see it as an honour for the firm (RPT).'*

He retired a few years later.

In 1975, the south side CTHJV office was only half occupied at this point, but more temporary offices were built to cater for the hundreds of engineers, administrators, commercial teams and workers yet to arrive.

The north side temporary offices were much smaller, catering for those working on the sills in the dry dock and later on Piers 1, 2 and 3, and the North Abutment. The offices were built on the original site of the Victorian Regent Tar Works, which had closed down and been acquired by the GLC, who quickly demolished it. There had been numerous factories in this area going back over a hundred years, which were razed as the developing industries using modern technologies took their place. In their day they had used an assortment of toxic chemicals and heavy metals, leaving a lethal legacy behind which you could occasionally smell seeping silently from the ground.

The river water was toxic too, and very few fish were seen in the 1970s. The River Thames had been polluted with discarded commercial waste from redundant industrial processes and sewage, and it would take decades to clean it up. Amazingly, by the time I left only five years later, the clean-up had made a noticeable improvement to the water quality, with fish starting to return, and you didn't need your stomach pumped if you fell in the river.

The CTHJV Construction Manager on the north side, was Ivor Morgan from Tarmac, who ruled the civils staff firmly, and was regularly seen on site every day. He was a small, tenacious, energetic Welshman in his forties who had a reputation for being hard but fair, and for giving support to the younger engineers when they arrived on site.

THE WATERMEN

After passing through the security gate, I was sent to the administration department. They were surprised to see me, and after giving me a safety helmet, decided I must have been allocated to the north side. I walked down to the sea wall, where the safety boats were moored, waiting to take personnel across the river. Each of these boats was crewed by a waterman, the majority of whom came from families from the East End of London who had worked on the river for generations.

The site was operating twenty-four hours a day, and the watermen were essential for all river transportation and manning the safety boats. They were led by the very capable and popular Frankie Barratt, a forty-five-year-old south Londoner who gave a disturbingly good impersonation of the actor Michael Caine. They were experts in reading the swirling twists and turns of old Father Thames, with currents renowned for changing from tranquil to deadly within a few metres. With their help and guidance, boat collisions were kept to a minimum, and no joint venture workers drowned in the river during the building of the barrier.

The Company of Watermen and Lightermen was founded in 1514, when the earliest Act of Parliament for regulating watermen, wherrymen and bargemen received Royal Assent from King Henry VIII. In 1780 the company moved into its own purpose-built hall in St Mary-At-Hill, Billingsgate, and is still there today. The Company is actively involved in the life of the river and those who work on it, and governed by a Court of Assistants led by The Master and four Wardens, who are still elected annually.

In the summer of 1975, CTHJV sponsored an 11km barge race from Greenwich to Westminster Bridge as part of the Greenwich Festival. Frankie Barrett chose one of the barges working on the site called 'The Black Cap', which was a heavy, 21-tonne registered vessel being used as a floating fuel carrier.

Each team consisted of four men plus an apprentice, and the CTHJV team had Frankie, Ronnie Fagan, Eddie Fagan, and Gerry Roberts, with Paul Evans the apprentice. The oars were massive, 7.7 metres long and weighing 27 kilograms each. It needed great skill and strength to manoeuvre the vessel. The cumbersome barge moved slowly, as it was positioned on the outside bend of the river. Shortly after the start, a tug, full of supporters, got too close and collided with it. After much cursing and swearing, and back-breaking effort, with skillful use of the currents they crept up to third place, and by half way, went into the lead, going on to win this gruelling race in three hours.

FIRST IMPRESSIONS

The short boat ride to the north side on this chilly November morning gave me the first glimpse of the site. It was a hive of activity and mind-numbing noise - from the screeching of the crane tracks, which manoeuvred the massive crawler cranes ponderously down the access jetties, to thundering pile hammers and pulsating generators, lit up by rainbows of angry sparks coming from the army of welders. The piling of the circular steel tubes for supports for the access jetty was making steady progress, stretching out from the south side like a legion of Roman soldiers, aiming for the centre of the river.

The tubes were connected by steel struts and bracings upon which sat thick, pre-cast reinforced concrete slabs to take the weight of the heaviest plant. Each pier would have a finger platform either side, going out at ninety degrees to the access way. The fingers either side of Pier 9 were complete and ready for the cranes to start the piling for the cofferdam. They used heavy, Larson, sheet piles up to 33 metres long, the largest of that type manufactured at that time. The piles were delivered in standard lengths to a temporary fabrication shop, set up adjacent to a nearby dock. Here they were welded to the required lengths and delivered by barge to site. The hammers were assembled to drive the sheet piles deep through the silt and brick-like Thanet sand, into the hard, flinty chalk below, which put up a violent resistance all the way. Some of the flints were substantial, over a metre in width.

On alighting the boat, I was greeted by a senior engineer who was puzzled why I had been sent to the north side, as I was not expected there either! Another engineer approached called Sam Cornberg, a man of short stature with a mass of hair and a mournful Mexican moustache, popular at the time. He was visibly suffering from the morning-after-the-night-before. He apologised profusely for disgracing himself the previous evening, which was brushed aside by his boss who said he hadn't even noticed. He then thought for a minute, looked at me intently, and asked if I drank. In those days it was unusual not to, and I nodded nervously in the affirmative.

He was pleased with that reply and immediately invited me to a competition that night where they were a man down. He swung round, satisfied with his find, and led me to a small office, where I was given some drawings and contract documents to look at. This was not the welcome I had expected, but it did give me fair warning of what lay ahead, and was also the start of a lifelong friendship with Sam.

By the end of the day it was confirmed I was going to work on the south side, so I did not have to be initiated into the north side competition, but it did give me an opportunity to see the scale of works to be carried out on the north bank. A large dry dock was under construction in shallow water using sheet piles enclosing the area for the sill casting beds for six sills and the construction of Piers 1 and 2.

Sheet piles needed to be driven on three sides of the dock in a rectangle 145 metres by 120 metres, with large, stepped berms forming an internal support for the piles on the inside of the dry dock. As much of the excavation as possible was done in the water by dredging, which was quicker than pumping, and spoil could be taken from the site by barge.

When the dry dock piling was complete, an extensive, three-stage well-point system was installed inside the dock on the berms to keep the water level down. The water was pumped out day and night, keeping the hundreds of workers safe inside the dock. Once the excavation was down to construction level, and was dry, concrete slabs would be cast to form the working base for casting the sills.

On returning to the south side I was shown the existing site organisation chart. The engineering activities were split into the marine works (we called the wet section), the concrete pier works (we called the dry section) and the sill works, which was based in the dry dock, each to be controlled by a Construction Manager. Each pier would eventually have a pier manager and a team of engineers and supervisors.

I was allocated to Pier 9 on the dry section and introduced to the pier manager, Gwyn Tennant, with whom I was to work for the next two years. He was a short, clean-shaven, salt and pepper hair, mixed-race Welshman from Cardiff, around thirty years old, full of serious, intense energy, and moved everywhere with short, rapid steps.

He gave me a warm welcome, a brief introduction, and a bundle of drawings of Pier 9 for me to acquaint myself with the details. There were thousands of drawings being produced by the consultant for the barrier, with many revisions ongoing, so it was essential to absorb large quantities of information quickly.

Blocks of portacabins were assembled near to the site and a few days later we moved into the first block. These were two-storey, mostly open-plan, with a few offices partitioned off, to maximise the number of staff. I grabbed a corner table, where there was shelf room for the many files that would be produced. Every table had a phone linking back to a switch-board and operator situated in the main office. Once the job got going there was constant noise, with a phone always ringing somewhere within the office.

In 1975 there were no computers in the offices, apart from a few small, handheld calculators, which were considered essential. These simple devices were soon more powerful than the computer on board the rocket that landed the first man on the moon in 1969. Some of the consultants were still using valve-operated calculators and punched-tape programmes. Fax machines were yet to be invented, and a small technology company called Microsoft had just been founded in California by a young upstart called Bill Gates. By the end of the project we heard the company word Apple for the first time.

THE PIER 9 TEAM

The following morning Gwyn called our small team into his office to bring us up to date. The piling for the cofferdam for Pier 9 had only just started, so it was still some weeks before the excavation would start, and months before it would be handed over to the Dry Section team.

This time was essential to check all the drawings, the planning for the building of the structures, and submission of the method statements to RPT for approval. This was a lot of work. At that time Pier 9 only had three engineers, including myself, and an experienced draughtsman who had yet to start. The other two engineers, both in their mid-twenties, were Dave Scott, a smart, ginger-haired, ambitious young graduate from the Home Counties, and Bob Trotter, a bespectacled bear of a man, with a mass of long, blonde hair and a magnificent, broad, soothing Yorkshire Dales brogue.

Each pier team had at least one draughtsman, essential for detailing both the permanent and temporary works. Martin Ash arrived the following week to start on Pier 9, after a full-size drawing board had been delivered for him. Computer Aided Design (CAD) was still years away. Some drawings were still being drawn on linen with ink and stencils, with prints taken off the original using an ammonia process, which certainly cleared your lungs.

The draughtsmen and women were nearly all from London draughting families who had been supplying skilled staff to the consultants in London for generations. Some of their drawings were masterpieces, with the printing for some in beautiful, copperplate script, and major components highlighted in watercolour.

Martin's job was a little simpler, but essential. The base level of the Pier 9 structure was twelve metres below the river bed, and would sit on a large plug of underwater concrete another 6 metres deep, covering the whole area inside the cofferdam. The finished structure would rise out of the river bed giving a total height of over 23 metres, the equivalent of a ten-storey office block sitting in the middle of the Thames.

Pier 9 was one of the smaller piers. The largest was 6 metres higher, standing an impressive 29 metres. The engineers would choose manageable, standardised pours around 3 metres high, and Martin would detail each level, drawn by hand.

Today, this can all be done in an instant using CAD software and the latest AI. It can spin the structure round 360 degrees, break it down, zoom in on tricky areas, check for clashes and make tiny, detailed changes, speeding up the whole process substantially. Traditional draughtsman's skills like Martin's died away overnight as computer power increased.

These detailed construction layouts became essential for the engineers and the different craftsmen working on the structure to see a visual image, and reduced any misinterpretation. Our engineers needed to study the consultant's drawings, look for errors, and any impracticalities, to see if changes were required before the formwork and the steel reinforcement was cut.

That day Gwyn took me on a guided trip along the access jetty pointing out the various stages of work being carried out, which was not always obvious. The CTHJV scope of work consisted of constructing nine piers named Pier 1 to Pier 9, strung out across the River Thames in a north/south direction, with an abutment at either end.

Eleven large, steel boxes of varying sizes composed of sheet piles were to be constructed to form cofferdams. They would be dewatered and each pier would be built inside it, in the dry. They needed to be built in two phases. P6 to P9 first, which would take four years, followed by a switch of navigation channels enabling P1-P5 to be completed.

All the six reinforced concrete sills will be built in the dry dock on the north bank, in two phases. Four will be built in the first phase, when the dock will be flooded and the sills floated out. The dock will then be dewatered, for the second phase, when the last two sills will be constructed, and floated out.

The access jetty had been pushed out towards the centre

of the river, and the finger platforms had been completed for Pier 9, with cranes assembling and driving the piles for the cofferdam. The south abutment cofferdam was complete and Pier 8 was close behind. Progress had been steady, but was behind schedule. Even though the enormous piles and pile hammers were substantial, the chalk bedrock gave particularly tough resistance, with large boulders of impregnable flint slowing down the rate of penetration, hard enough to buckle the bottom of some of the piles.

After the cofferdam was complete, substantial strutting frames had to be installed to resist the immense water pressure. The majority of the frames were underwater, so specialist divers were employed to install them before excavation could commence. This was particularly difficult because visibility was minimal and the divers were often working by touch. Nothing was going to be easy on this project, but it did look as though our team on Pier 9 was going to have a little more time for the planning and preparation before descending to the bottom of a dry cofferdam.

On returning to the office, Gwyn allocated me the task of checking the steel reinforcement drawings, to raise any queries with the consultant, and plan the large numbers of steel cutting schedules for the cutting and bending yard. Due to the thousands of tonnes of steel reinforcement required, it had been decided to set up our own steel yard and cut and bend the steel ourselves, which would make last-minute changes easy to deal with.

The steel would be ordered direct from the manufactures; at that time we used British Steel, and it would be delivered to site by a constant convoy of heavy lorries, each with a 40-tonne load. Experienced steel supervisors were appointed on either side, but things did not quite go as planned, as we were to discover around a year later.

Thousands of drawings were issued by the consultant over the next few months, and for the rest of the year I was hunched over my desk, firing off hundreds of queries to the consultant, putting together steel schedules, and helping Martin construct his jigsaw puzzle as we examined every minute detail of the structure. I would try to take a break once a day and go for a walk on site along the access platforms, watching the welders at work, and the piling hammers making slow progress through the river bed, driving the piles for the cofferdams.

I was also hearing the rumblings of discontent coming from the workforce, who were talking of strikes in the New Year.

4

1976

During 1975, the site was working two twelve-hour shifts for five days a week, with the weekends used for plant maintenance and catching up in specific areas where slippage had occurred. Although this gave the workforce an opportunity to earn good money with overtime, they valued their leisure time, so it was only a small proportion that worked a sixty-hour week. As a result, productivity was low, and with the increasing number of technical problems with the piling and excavation, for which the joint venture design team were seeking solutions, progress was faltering. Work in the north dry dock however, steamed ahead, where working conditions were more conventional.

To add to these pressures, there were problems with extra design checks required on the supports for the piling rigs, which were box girders. These checks were introduced into the UK following major accidents with box girder bridges in Britain, Germany and Australia in the early seventies. The checks on site, supervised by RPT, resulted in additional strengthening being added to piling rig supports. Welders had to carry out the additional work over water, which allowed them to claim a plus rate, and boosted their earnings considerably. Paul Sivey, a young CTHJV engineering manager on the north side, was given the challenging job of negotiating the rates with the union representative.

Paul was born in London, but spent his childhood in Hong Kong, Japan, Sri Lanka and Jamaica, before studying at Queen Mary College, London University for a degree in Civil Engineering. He joined Costain Civil Engineering in 1973 as a site engineer, working on motorways in the UK, before going to Dubai to help build the tunnel under the creek. Later, courtesy of Costain, he continued his studies for a year to gain an MSc in Construction Management at Loughborough. He was transferred to the barrier in the autumn of 1975, working on the north side for the beginning of the sill construction.

One Friday afternoon, Paul sat down with the welders' union representative, a large, intimidating character with some impressive scars and a distinct lack of humour. Paul went through his calculations for that week and presented the rate to the impassive character sat opposite, who stared at him intently. He rejected Paul's figure and came back with double the amount. Paul offered the carefully worked out figures again and received the same reply, this time a little more forcibly, and was asked if his family was well. Paul looked at his rather unfriendly expression, and quickly glanced at the figures again. After a short pause, Paul announced that there was a possibility of some flexibility, which could improve the offer slightly. It was immediately rejected by the welder's representative, who gave no hint of possibly lowering his figure.

Paul inquired where the welders' figure had come from. The reply was blunt 'It is always that amount'. When Paul explained that he had a problem justifying the figures with his senior manager, he was greeted with a heavy sigh.

The negotiator stood up, pulled out what appeared to be a gun from his jacket, and slowly, without saying a word, placed it on the table, looking at him menacingly. Paul had not come across this scenario during his MA studies, or even during his time in Jamaica. His blood pressure was rising rapidly, and he swiftly ended the meeting, saying he would see what he could do. Returning to his office, he considered what he could possibly have done to have deserved this job, and if he should be asking for a plus rate as well.

In 1976, Warren Hibbs arrived on site, and later that year took over from John Lofthouse as the Marine Works Construction Manager. Paul became his deputy, forming a very fruitful partnership, completing the building of the sills and the planning of the tow-outs from the dry dock. Paul left the barrier in 1982 to join Costain Construction on large building projects, culminating in leading the City of London unit, before a successful period with Costain International, including a spell in Zimbabwe, and as MD of the international division, where his negotiation experiences on the barrier came in particularly useful.

UNION DISPUTES

This had been a turbulent period in UK politics. Petrol prices had trebled in 1973, and with the coal strikes and subsequent power cuts leading to a three-day week, it was the end of the line for the Conservative Ted Heath government. Labour won the election, with Harold Wilson returning as Prime Minister, and promising a pro-union policy. Their time in government did not start well, with the coal miners demanding and getting a 35% pay deal.

In 1975, inflation had reached its high point of 24.2%, and unemployment soared to 1.25 million, so the unions were in a confident and militant mood, demanding ever higher wages to cover the increasing cost of living. Strikes were commonplace and this period was seen as the high-water mark of trade union influence. When Wilson resigned in 1976 due to ill health. Jim Callaghan took over until 1979. He lost the general election to Margaret Thatcher, who swept into power, eager to take the powerful union barons head on.

Over the next two years, the barrier acquired an unfair reputation for continuous union disputes, but walk-outs were uncommon, and partial stoppages were by relatively few men. No account was taken of the complexity of the labour relations.

At that time, John Friel was the union convener and a member of the Union of Construction, Allied Trades and Technicians (UCATT). He did not have an easy job, as he represented all union parties. There were at least five unions, all with very different backgrounds, and the welders were a good example. Many were members of the Amalgamated Society of Boilermakers, Shipwrights, Blacksmiths and Structural Workers (ASBSBSW), who didn't accept lay-offs easily, but which was common practice for the civil engineering unions. When four welders were made redundant, it led to an eight-week stoppage by the other welders, but work continued on the rest of the site. The watermen were in the water section of the Transport and General Workers Union (TGWU), and came under a separate agreement.

HBM, the Dutch contingent of CTHJV was generally not familiar with the British way of working, and in John Reeve's words, (the Costain Managing Director), 'They were thrown into the deep end of UK industrial relations.'

This tended to harden their attitude to disputes, which complicated matters further. By and large, the consortium had the support of officials for 90% of the time, and union officials were kept fully informed on the progress of the renegotiation of the contract in 1976. However, it still didn't stop overtime bans and partial stoppages, which had a serious effect on productivity. The major strike did not come until 1977.

EXCAVATING THE COFFERDAMS

In early 1976, the Pier 9 sheet piling for the cofferdam was completed, and the first of four large, internal frames was fitted. It was positioned close to the top of the sheet pile and was the only frame above the water level. Heavy struts were fitted to the frame across the cofferdam to resist the huge water pressure. Packing, made of fabric bags filled with sand, cement and a grout additive, filled the variable gaps between the sheet piles and the walings. The excavation commenced once the top frame was fitted, and the remaining three frames were installed underwater as the excavation proceeded. It was a slow, laborious job in almost zero visibility.

The thick alluvium (silt) was removed by a grab, which was suspended by steel cables from a crawler crane, without too many problems. When it reached the harder areas of Thanet sand and the chalk, it was hoped to use a new, rotating cutter-section drill that had been brought from Japan. It had gone through extensive trials in Tokyo, and the plant experts had been convinced it would be up to the job. Successful trials were carried out on a similar band of chalk at West Thurrock, Essex, but when it got to the Thames, it quickly became apparent it was unable to deal with the large, solid flint deposits in the unusually hard chalk under this part of the river.

After the silt and softer levels of the Thanet sand were removed, the drill was lowered down by crane through the murky water, and the rotating cutters attempted to grip the undulating surface of the chalk. When the drill came to the flint-filled levels of chalk, it refused to grip and bounced around like a demented octopus, much to the despair and frustration of the plant manager. After weeks of futile attempts, the drill was removed, put into storage, covered by a large tarpaulin, and quietly sold. Over the next few months, trials were carried out using a wide variety of other equipment. It was found that pre-drilling the chalk and using large, clam-shell grabs suspended by steel ropes from a crane was the most effective solution.

A regular pattern of holes was drilled through the chalk to break it up, for removal by a Kelly grab. Large, 1200mm-diameter augers (drills) were attached to cranes to drill down to the formation level, where the underwater concrete would be poured. When the formation level was almost reached, a 250mm-diameter air-lift was used to suction up the debris to form a clean formation level. Divers from RPT were then sent down in a diving bell to carry out probe tests on the surface of the chalk and install settlement indicators, which would measure how much settlement had occurred after the underwater concrete had been poured.

The Kelly grabs scooped the chalk with powerful hydraulic jaws, and dropped the contents into barges moored alongside the cofferdam. The barges were towed downriver for disposal in a reclamation area, a continuous fleet moving up and down the river twenty-four hours a day.

The shoulders of chalk caught in the profile of the sheet piles were also removed, and the chalk underneath the struts. Various methods were used, starting with heavy chisels, which were slid down the inside panel of the piles. A device called the boot was used for the chalk under the struts. It crumpled dramatically with the first attempt, but the deluxe version was a triumph. Divers were also employed using hydrojet lances working from a cradle, which was slow and time consuming. As a result, it was decided to trial explosives for Pier 8. Controlled blasting, with gelignite charges, was successfully used, and this was the method adopted for the rest of the piers.

A recurring problem was that every time the tide rolled in, twice a day, it brought a thick layer of fine river silt from the estuary down-river which seeped into the cofferdam through gaps in the clutches of the piles. An air-lift suctioned the silt into barges moored alongside the cofferdam, where it settled out for disposal.

It had been a hectic year for the marine section, and it gained a reputation for innovation and invention of devices coming out of the welding shop, but the pressure was still on. During this period, John Lofthouse, Chris Gane and the marine section team developed air-lifting techniques, from the small, 100mm-diameter air-lifts normally used by the divers, to crane handle 900mm-diameter air-lifts complete with mobile discharge chutes spanning the cofferdams. This used a lot of compressed air, but it worked!

Around this time, in the summer of 1976, a new manager arrived to join the marine section. Warren Hibbs was in his early thirties, a tall, highly experienced and amiable high-flyer, who came to the barrier as the deputy to the Marine Manager, John Lofthouse, with whom he had worked a few years earlier in Gravesend. Warren was to become a key member of the new team, and was a major contributor to the success of the barrier.

Warren was born in Kingston upon Thames in 1945 and was brought up in London. He studied at Leeds University and graduated with a degree in Civil Engineering in 1967. He joined J. Mowlem, a major contractor at the time, as a graduate indentured engineer, and started work on site on an extension to the container dock at Tilbury, which had played such a major part in the escalation of the closure of London Docks. Following this, he was seconded to a consultant, John Taylor, who specialised in Public Health Engineering, to give him the design experience to become chartered.

In 1970 he joined Costain Civil Engineering as a site engineer, working on a variety of motorway projects at the beginning of the motorway boom. He also worked on a gas pipeline project at Gravesend with John Lofthouse, increasing his marine experience. His final job before being transferred to the barrier was on the Liskeard by-pass in Cornwall, from where he brought some of his best supervisors, including Ken Hodge, a fine Cornishman with a magnificent West Country drawl, and a wry sense of humour.

John Lofthouse had requested that Warren join the marine section, and Warren arrived when the marine works were struggling to make progress. After six months, John became ill and was unable to continue. He left the project and Warren was unexpectedly promoted to one of the most challenging positions on the barrier, as Marine Works Construction Manager.

For the next six years he would be tested to the limit across all aspects of the marine works. He built a team that worked together well.

Gavin Maxwell-Hart and John Hudson covered the excavation of the cofferdams, and Chris Gane looked after the divers and strutting in the cofferdams.

Chris was in his twenties, a talented engineer with a fine sense of humour, whose greatest pleasure was solving engineering problems, and creating complicated windups. He stayed with Costain for the rest of his career, rising up through the ranks to become Chief Engineer of Costain Civil Engineering some twenty years later. I had the pleasure of meeting up with him again in 2019. Sadly, he died the following year.

Warren worked closely with the HBM engineers. Aarvid Degonaars and Wim Van Est were key members of the marine section team, particularly on the sill activities. HBG (the HBM parent company) piling rigs were also used on the south side cofferdams, and also used for the installation and removal of the access jetties. HBM contributed valuable lessons learnt from extensive experience in marine works.

The marine section supervised the installation and removal of the cofferdams, access jetties and the circular fairing cells (used to protect the cofferdams from possible collisions) as well as the dry dock installation, and reinstatement after the sills float-out. It also covered the excavations for Piers 1 and 2 inside the dry dock, the sill tow-outs, and the sand flow bedding for the sills. Also, the bed protection after the sills were lowered into position. All in all, a very challenging scope of work for Warren and his team.

With the unique experience Warren gained on the barrier, it set him up for ever-more challenging projects with increasing responsibility. He stayed until the barrier was operational, and in 1982, accepted a position with Costain West Africa to go to Lagos as Contracts Manager. He would be the UK liaison for the Oyo Water Scheme, one of the largest in Africa, which I also happened to be working on, and pushed for the completion of the Iwopin paper and pulp mill, both challenging projects in a very difficult country to work in.

He returned to the UK in 1986, and was appointed Managing Director of Haig and Ringrose, a Costain subsidiary in Middlesborough, where he restored profitability, and in 1991 became a Regional Director of Edmund Nuttall for Scotland and the North-East on a variety of harbour projects. In 2004 he returned to

Costain, and was appointed Project Director of a Costain/ China Harbour Joint Venture to work in Mexico, building a large offshore break-water in 23-meter water depths formed from caissons larger than the Thames Barrier sill units. There he negotiated a myriad of challenges, including coping with the behaviour of large whales, and dealing with the idiosyncrasies of the Pacific Ocean.

Rick Randall and Paul Sivey were also brought to this project, reuniting the barrier team after twenty-two years.

After returning to the UK Head Office in 2006, Warren worked on a variety of tenders, before taking up consultancy work, and finally retired to Yorkshire in 2012.

THE DIVERS

CTHJV awarded all the diving works on the barrier to Shiers Diving Contracts in 1975. The company was founded by Don Shiers, a hugely experienced diver, and innovative and charismatic man. His company was based at Hemsby Hall, at Great Yarmouth, in Norfolk, and had been closely involved during the tender advising Costain. At its peak, the barrier was operating three eight-hour shifts, requiring nine teams of divers using 126 personnel, with Bill McKean and John Shaw as the diving superintendents. There was also a diving medical consultant, Dr. John King, who was employed to carry out checks and look after the welfare of the divers. At one point there were more divers working on the barrier than on all the oil rigs in the North Sea.

Don Shiers designed a purpose-built diving bell for the barrier, which was open at the bottom, and illuminated and linked by radio. Two divers could enter the bell from the top when it was out of the water, and be lowered down for the inspections after the excavation was completed. Any testing required could be carried out to ensure that conditions were right for the underwater concrete to be poured.

The divers were allowed to work for a maximum of four hours before resurfacing, when they had to go into a thera-peutic decompression chamber. A two-storey block was used for the rest area. Shiers' divers also played an important role in the sinking and positioning of the sills and the removal of the temporary works, and were an essential part of the inspection team.

RPT employed a separate team of divers from Strongwork Diving International, who worked closely with Shiers, to super-vise all diving inspection operations and provided a back-up service to the team of six RPT engineer-divers.

UNDERWATER CONCRETE

The south abutment had been having problems with the exca-vation in their cofferdam, and it was Pier 9 that was the first structure ready to receive the underwater concrete plug. Over 5000m^3 of concrete (sufficient to fill St Paul's Cathedral dome), were poured in one continuous operation over three days and nights in June 1976.

The planning had started in 1975, when trial mixes were tested to examine the flow characteristics of the concrete and the retardation required. We were going to carry out the largest underwater concrete pour in the world at that time, so there was more than a hint of excitement, and trepidation.

The setting of concrete is a complex chemical reaction, and oddly, the perfect setting environment is under water. It sets quickly in these conditions and needs to have retardant added to slow down the setting time to enable it to keep flowing. A large amount of heat is generated in the formation of concrete from the cement and aggregate, and to reduce this, 50% of the cementitious content is pulverised fuel ash (PFA). In addition, the concrete would be pumped, a factor which had to be taken into account in the mix design. Trials were carried out in the concrete laboratory under the supervision of the concrete manager, Clive Carden, who was able to achieve the ideal concrete mix required on site.

New engineers were arriving every week, including Alistair Handford, a young, talented and ambitious civil engineer. He joined us on Pier 9 for the underwater concrete pour, and was eager to participate in this unique experience. He became another lifelong friend, and twenty years later we met up in Hong Kong when we were working on two major bridges adjacent to each other serving the new airport.

Alistair Handford was born in Gatley, near Manchester, and was raised in the Wirral. He studied engineering at Cambridge University, and specialised in civil engineering subjects in his third year. He was interviewed by Costain in his last year, and was impressed by the training the company gave to graduates, which seemed the fastest route to becoming chartered and obtaining his MICE.

His first job was on a motorway, the start for so many young engineers. His was the A329M Wokingham by-pass, where he learned how to put his theory into practice. He then took a few months off when he had the opportunity to visit Nigeria, and travelled by motor bike from Ibadan to Kano, experiencing his first colourful taste of living overseas. He was to visit Ibadan twenty-five years later, and sadly, did not notice a huge difference.

He was seconded to the famous consulting engineers, Sir William Halcrow and Partners, to gain design experience, and was surprised to find himself checking a Costain cofferdam design for a tunnel in Dubai.

Alistair transferred to the Thames Barrier in 1975 and joined the Pier 9 team working on the preparations for the underwater concrete pour. He worked on the night shift during the pour, measuring the rate of flow of the concrete with frozen fingers at three o'clock in the morning. He considered it a dark art that mysteriously worked! After Pier 9, he became a key member of the dry section team, working on many of the piers. He has many vivid memories of working on the superstructure of Pier 9 in the middle of winter, exposed to the bitterly cold Siberian winds, and working on the substructure of later piers at the bottom of the cofferdams, just occasionally catching a glimpse of blue, summer sky.

He was rewarded for his efforts and was promoted to Pier Manager of Pier 3, (identical to Pier 9). Due to all the experience gained up to that point, Alistair was able to break all records on the pier, and led his team to finish comfortably ahead of the Key Date requirement.

In 1981, Alistair was transferred to Costain Construction and worked on a variety of large projects in London, culminating as Project Manager building Barclays' new head office in Lombard Street, which was dubbed 'The Jukebox'. At this time he was also working with the Prince's Trust, and became an advisor for building projects with Operation Raleigh in Peru.

In 1994, at very short notice, he was asked to go to Hong Kong to take over as Project Manager of a Joint Venture with Mitsui for the building of the Tsing Ma Bridge, one of the longest road/rail suspension bridges in the world at that time. It was a key part of the link to the new airport, and on a very tight schedule aiming to finish by 1997. Cleveland Bridge were fabricating and erecting the steel deck and sidespans, and Alistair met up again with Dick Thorp, who had done such a good job on the erection of the gates on the barrier. All the contractual dates were met, and the project was a success.

Alistair stayed on in Hong Kong as Hong Kong Director and Managing Director of South-East Asia, to tender for more infrastructure work that was due to start in the next five years.

He returned to London and was appointed to the Costain Executive Board with a variety of roles including Group Director for PFI projects and Investments, until he retired to Buckinghamshire in 2012.

For the Pier 9 underwater concrete, there were twenty-four tremie pipes, spaced in pairs equally down the length of the cofferdam, with two pipes at a time used to pour the concrete into the cofferdam. As the concrete rose, the pipes could not be lifted too quickly or they would lose their seal in the concrete. Too slowly and the pipe could be stuck fast in the setting concrete. Monitoring was made by regularly dipping blindly into the murky water inside the cofferdam to check the level of the rising concrete, and that the slope of the leading edge of the concrete was running at the right angle to keep driving the silt forward. Not easy, especially at three o'clock on a freezing, winter night shift.

The concrete was delivered from the site batcher in relatively small concrete skip lorries (to keep the weight down on the access jetty), to concrete pumps on the access jetty. Continuous supply of concrete materials to the batcher was critical. The cement was delivered directly from Blue Circle, and the PFA was delivered by rail from large, coal-fired power stations all over England and Wales. Due to the quantities involved, we had our own temporary railway siding at Silvertown, on the north side.

Materials had to be delivered by lorries twenty-four hours a day through the streets of south-east London, and by river barges, so it was essential close liaison was kept with the Metropolitan Police, the river police, the water board, electricity board and local councils. There were also lengthy negotiations with the union representatives on extra bonus payments, to guarantee there were no labour problems.

Allowances had to be made for delays and breakdowns, so stand-by equipment was essential. This included concrete pumps and trucks, generators, cranes and lengths of 300mm-diameter tremie pipes. The operatives, electricians, mechanics and managers of the plant department, led by Ron Woodhatch, were key to keeping everything going.

PRESSURE RELIEF SYSTEM

Incredibly, the weight of the underwater concrete placed was still not heavy enough to resist the uplift water pressures generated when the cofferdams were de-watered. So, a pressure relief system consisting of long metal tubes were installed under the underwater concrete.

The number and details of the tubes varied for each pier - Pier 9 had twenty 865mm-diameter tubes cast vertically into the underwater concrete. Before dewatering the cofferdam, the pipes were drilled out to a depth of ten metres below river bed level, and filled with gravel. The ground water would push up from below, and be fed into a perimeter drainage system, where it would be pumped out. The wells were eventually capped when sufficient concrete had been placed into the structure to achieve the necessary dead weight, which was greater than the uplift of the water pressure.

Despite all these problems, the underwater concrete for Pier 9 was poured successfully in June, with materials delivered in time, without bringing east London to a standstill. The batchers coped with three days' continuous working, and no concrete pumps broke down. The tremie pipe system worked relatively smoothly, the concrete did not overheat after pouring, and the cores taken afterwards showed there had been an almost perfect joint made with the underlying chalk. It was a real tribute to all those involved, and the celebrations went on late into the night at our local Trumans pub on the corner of Eastmoor Street, *The Victoria*, that we had renamed *The Barrier Arms*.

SOME LIKE IT HOT

What we couldn't anticipate was that 1976 was due to be the hottest summer of the 20th century.

It had been a very dry autumn in 1975, with little rain in the spring of 1976. This continued until June 23, when drought was officially declared. As a result, a Minister of Drought (Dennis Howell) was appointed. Between June 22 and July 7, every day somewhere in the UK exceeded 32°C, with devastating heath and forest fires. On July 3 it reached 35.9°C in Cheltenham, and on August 6 the Drought Act was passed, with hose pipes banned, (households were encouraged to report anyone in the street using them!). By August 31 London had only ninety days of water supply left, tarmac was melting on the roads, and the temperature on the London underground was a sweltering 37°C. There was no air-conditioning on the trains or in cars, with only cinemas and some bars having such a luxury.

To keep the temperature of the concrete down, the storage containers for the cement and aggregate were painted white, (a practice usually only necessary in the Middle East) and plans were drawn up to add ice to the water. The men on site were given water rations, and a few times ice lollies were given out to the workforce.

To add to their discomfort, massive swarms of seven-spotted ladybirds started to arrive in the south of the country in June. By late July, there were an estimated 23.65 billion of them swarming across southern and eastern England. They covered the offices and jetties on site, and rumours were rife they had a poisonous bite.

One young engineer, Neil Truphet recounted he was travelling back from Scotland in his car and pulled over for a rest near London. He pulled the sunroof back and nodded off. On awakening, to his horror, he thought he was in a Hitchcock film when he found that he and the interior of his small saloon were smothered in tens of thousands of ladybirds!

The drought lasted another month and officially finished on August 27.

ICE COLD IN WOOLWICH

Work on Pier 8 was catching up on Pier 9 due to the improved excavation methods used, and the underwater concrete was poured in December 1976. It was bitterly cold. A vicious, easterly wind blowing up the Thames from Siberia was bone-chilling, and a marked contrast to the hot weather experienced a few months earlier on Pier 9. I was working on the night shift, and we made sure we all had at least four layers of clothing on. The day shift had gone well with a smooth handover, but it was getting colder. First came rain, then sleet and finally, around midnight, flurries of icy snow. With the temperature now well below freezing, the delivery of the concrete was slowing down, and the operators, labourers, and engineers checking the concrete levels were desperately trying to remember what summer had been like.

After the experience of Pier 9, we decided to rig up some speakers and broadcast Radio Caroline, one of the early pirate radio stations which tended to play rock 'n roll and pop music throughout the night. It would not disturb anyone, being well away from habitation, and would boost morale on cold, winter nights.

On the first particularly cold night, someone rang in to make a request for all those pouring underwater concrete on the Thames Barrier. A popular song around that time was called *Chanson d'Amour* by the group Manhattan Transfer. It eventually reached number one in the UK and Ireland hit parades. With the snow and icy sleet flurries driving in horizontally, one of the Irish labourers, waiting for the next concrete delivery, started singing the song's catchy refrain. Next thing he suddenly broke into a dance routine using his shovel as a cane, in true Fred Astaire fashion. Within a minute, six more joined in, singing and dancing in unison with their shovels in a kind of crazy, Busby Berkeley routine. The sound of music, and raucous laughter echoed across the Thames. It was five minutes of magic, not to be forgotten, and got us through the rest of that shift.

THE REVIEW

In July 1976, the review negotiations of the main civil contract opened with the client, which had been agreed at the original signing. The GLC was unhappy with the progress of the CTH Joint Venture. Work had slipped six months behind the original schedule after just eighteen months, despite the temporary works for the southern half of the river being virtually complete and the first underwater concrete pour completed successfully. At that current rate of progress, it would take another seven years to complete, and that was totally unacceptable to the client.

Termination of the contract was given serious consideration, but the cost of termination, possible litigation, and re-tendering costs made no economic sense. Plus there was a very real chance of bankrupting two of the biggest contractors in the UK. In any case, who else would be capable of delivering such a complex project? A new consortium would have to go through a similar learning curve as CTHJV, and with the risks and challenges now better understood, the bids would come in substantially more expensive. Better to negotiate with the devil you know, and explore what improvements could be made. The negotiations were prolonged, detailed and sometimes fraught, with serious financial implications for all parties if an agreement could not be reached.

It was agreed that CTHJV would be paid net audited costs for the first two years, with a revision of contract rates increased by 16% for future works. A lump sum payment was to cover the cost of industrial disputes for the two years up to the summer of 1978, and included a limitation of profit and loss clauses. Despite the contract rates being enhanced by some 16%, CTHJV had not managed to make a profit by 1978.

CHANGES

Part of the new agreement was that there should be a re-organisation of CTHJV management, starting with the Project Manager. As a result, John Grice was appointed to replace David Derbyshire, who returned to head office.

David was smart and had done his best in extremely difficult circumstances, but RPT considered him too young for this position, with not enough experience to deal with such a challenging project, and wanted a change.

John was an experienced Director of Costain Civil Engineering, in his late forties, and had been in charge of the Midlands office in Coventry. John Reeve, a senior director of Costain, was also brought in to be more closely involved with the problems on site. They were expected to review work practices, boost productivity, and get the contract back on target. After further difficult negotiations with the client and consultant, a final agreement was signed on November 11 1976. This added 40% to the price of the contract at 1973 prices, which the Ministry of Agriculture, Fisheries and Food (MAFF) had the unenviable task of explaining to the Parliamentary Public Accounts Committee.

It tended to be Costain policy to move senior managers on from large sites after two or three years. They would have been working long hours in stressful conditions, and it was easy to get burnt out. A change of scene gave them a chance to recharge their batteries.

David Derbyshire had made a major contribution to the early planning and design stages of the project. With the site set up and construction well under way, it was time for a more hands-on approach. As the piers began to take shape, the extensive experience of John Grice would be required.

David Hoare was also moved on shortly afterwards by Tarmac. He was posted abroad and sadly, died of a heart attack a few years later in Egypt. He was replaced by Brian Georgel, who came down from the Midlands, and was a more experienced manager with a less flamboyant style, preferred by the traditionalists at RPT.

By the end of 1976, progress was picking up on site, but was still slow. Pier 9 and the south abutment were under construction,

Pier 8 had completed the underwater concrete pour, but Pier 7 was struggling with the excavation. On the north side, the dry dock was complete and the construction of the sills was going smoothly. The client review was complete, a new agreement with CTHJV was finalized, and a fresh, senior management team was in place to drive the contract forward through the next stages of construction.

However, agreement with the unions had yet to be settled.

5

1977 – PART 1

A NEW LEADER

In 1977, John Reeve, Chairman of the CTH Joint Venture, was responsible for bringing John Grice to the barrier as the new Project Manager. He knew it required a special man with exceptional skills to overcome the unique problems that he would have to deal with.

He wanted to minimise the financial and commercial burden on John, to enable him to concentrate entirely on the construction, technical and site problems. He appointed a senior commercial manager, John South, to take over the commercial activities, and brought in another senior manager from Head Office, David Staines, to spearhead the industrial relations. As a highly experienced chartered civil and structural engineer, John Grice was more than capable of handling the technical side, but it was his personality, tenacity, enormous energy, and an ability to lead from the front by example that was going to make the difference.

John Robert Grice was born in Salford on June 24, 1928. On the west side of Greater Manchester, close to the

Manchester Ship canal, Salford had been an important industrial and commercial centre during the Industrial Revolution. In 1929 a long, global recession started, which sent the city into a decade of decline, which John would have witnessed whilst growing up with his sister and two brothers. The hard times experienced in the north were evocatively captured in the famous industrial paintings of the matchstick figures of L S Lowry.

John's father, Robert Grice, was a skilled machinist working for Metropolitan-Vickers (Metrovick) in their large factory at Trafford Park, Manchester. In 1928, Metrovick was a major electrical engineering company, manufacturing a wide variety of heavy electrical equipment and engines, and the factory was one of the most important engineering facilities in Britain. In the 1930s recession, everyday life was a struggle, which would have been felt in the Grice family. In 1938, as war approached, Metrovick had a boost when it was awarded a contract to work with the Air Ministry on radar and prototype turboprop engines with the brilliant inventor, Frank Whittle. As war approached, more contracts were awarded to build heavy bombers at the factory, including the famous Lancaster bomber, enabling Robert to keep working while raising his young family.

This experience would have given John an early understanding of the importance and variety of engineering from an early age. In 1939, it was apparent that Manchester was going to be an obvious target for the Luftwaffe, so the older children were evacuated to a safer part of England before the bombing started. The factory was bombed in December 1940, but the family returned to Salford in time for John to finish his schooling.

John was a good student, but as with so many young people at that time, he left school in 1944 aged 16 to earn a little money to help contribute to the household. He became an articled pupil with J. Gerrard and Sons, a Building and Civil Engineering contractor based in Manchester.

The company had plenty of work rebuilding the damage caused by the war, including roads, housing, office blocks and a power station. John worked during the day and studied at night school to pass his exams for entry to Manchester University in 1949, where he studied for a degree in Civil Engineering. He graduated with a BSc. (Hons) in 1953, and joined Holst & Co, structural and civil engineers based in Watford, Hertfordshire.

For the next seven years he gained design and construction experience on a variety of civil and structural projects in the north-west of England. These included factories, power stations, colliery buildings and reservoirs. He showed an impressive talent for the design of a wide variety of structures, including the complexities of a cooling tower for a power station. His ability was recognised and he was promoted from section leader to deputy chief engineer, still in his early thirties.

During this time, he met and married his wife Ena, and they had two sons, Michael and Philip, both of whom went on to become civil engineers. In 1960, he returned to J. Gerrard for two years as a senior site manager, and went back to Holst in 1962 as an area manager, where he was in charge of a group of design and construct contracts.

The final contract with Holst was to design and build a brand new power station, the Collette Power Station in St Helier, Jersey, and in 1963 he took his family to live there. The thermal power station was oil-fired with a capacity of 30MW, located on the harbour, and had many design challenges. It has a tall, distinctive chimney that still dominates the skyline of St Helier today. The intake structure for the cooling water required a cofferdam to be built in the sea, which gave him invaluable marine and cofferdam experience for his later work on the Thames Barrier. Work started in 1963 and by 1966 the power station was successfully commissioned. He was now approaching forty years old, with a wide range of experience, and was ambitious. He was ready to move on to further challenges.

In 1967, John saw opportunities with Costain Construction, and joined as an area manager. He started in the Leeds office which covered Yorkshire and Scotland, and then moved to the busy Coventry office to manage a wide variety of major building projects across the Midlands.

When John Reeve offered him the position of Project Manager on the Thames Barrier, one of the largest and most prestigious contracts in the UK at that time, he was not fazed by the challenge. Looking back later he commented,

'I was used to dealing with unions in the Manchester and Liverpool environment, so the Thames Barrier, with its

highly complicated union situation, was not that alarming.
But it was difficult by any standards. The important thing
was to tell the union leaders what you want and give them
an opportunity to do it, or to make their minds up whether
they would or would not co-operate. But at least you tell
them.'

When John moved to London and took up the position on the barrier in the autumn of 1977, he started as he meant to go on. He had a different approach to all problems. His aim in solving them was to get the best brains available around the table and work as late as necessary to thrash out a solution. With the unions, he wanted to involve the full time officials of the main unions in establishing a way to negotiate and avoid conflict. He kept to this plan with the many problems that arose, and on the whole, it worked well.

First, he brought in a highly experienced and efficient senior secretary, June Kramer, to manage the many meetings and people he was going to have to deal with. This enabled him to spend more time on site. He would regularly be seen striding along the access jetties towards the piers first thing in the morning, accompanied by senior supervisor, Gary Bamber to check over any problems that might have arisen, with Terry Parrot, the senior supervisor on the night shift, and the pier managers.

They would talk through any issues with the managers and supervisors immediately, understand where the problems were, and discuss what improvements could be made. He quickly realised that the main weakness was lack of communication between the shifts, and that there were too many breaks in a two, twelve-hour shift system, resulting in the loss of hours of productivity a day. A three, eight-hour shift pattern would be much more efficient and productive, as long as there were good handovers at the end of each shift. This would no longer make the night shift a ghost shift, but make it fully operational.

After consultation with the other consortium partners, he proposed this radical change to RPT and the GLC. They agreed and swiftly found approval with the Ministry of Agriculture, Food and Fisheries, and surprisingly among the union leaders. However, they expressed concern about the high unemployment in the area, and that the increase in the number of shifts would lead to a 50% increase in the labour force on site.

This did not go down well with the existing workforce, as it would mean a considerable loss of overtime earnings. Long and frustrating negotiations started in early 1977, and despite the introduction of a generous shift allowance, agreement could not be reached. CTHJV therefore imposed the three-shift working pattern, (which it was entitled to do), with compulsory handovers at the end of each shift. Recruitment had been going on for months and new labour had started arriving for the new shift system. The benefits were never clearly seen at this point, and a series of partial stoppages and restricted working practices by the existing labour ensued.

Weeks went by and there was still no agreement. This inevitably forced an all-out stoppage for two months, starting in May 1977.

NEW FACES

Adrian Franklin had arrived from Costain Civil Engineering in the spring of 1976, and replaced Ralph Pesticcio from Tarmac as Construction Manager of the south side permanent works. He would lead the much-needed new staff that were about to arrive and fill the new block of temporary offices being built.

Adrian John Douglas Franklin was born in Jerusalem in 1944 which, at that time, was part of Palestine. His father had been working there for many years, but as the situation deteriorated in the lead up to the formation of Israel, the family moved to Lagos, Nigeria in 1947. It was a radically different culture, where he lived the life of a privileged colonial, in an era that was drawing to a close.

There, for the first time, he saw a bulldozer in action, creating a clearing through a jungle for a new road. The contractor building the road was Costain West Africa, with whom he was to reacquaint himself many years later. This image stayed with him, and he believes was a factor that steered him towards a career in civil engineering.

A few years later, Adrian returned to England to start his schooling at Kent College in Canterbury, which must have been a little bland after his early experiences abroad. In 1963, he was offered a place at Sheffield University to study for a degree in Civil and Structural Engineering. However, he wanted to see more of the world first, and so took a gap year with Voluntary Service Overseas (VSO), and was sent to teach at a Chinese school in Sarawak in a remote part of Borneo. This was yet another new culture for him, and good experience for the challenges he would face later in life.

He graduated from Sheffield in 1967, and his

first job was based in London, working with Costain on international projects in their design office. They included the first cross-harbour tunnel in Hong Kong, early port projects in Dubai and a new airport in the Seychelles. In the following eight years, he became chartered and expanded his site experience on a variety of projects. They started with submarine bases in Coulport and Plymouth, continued with a breakwater in Swansea, jetty extensions at Sheerness, and new fuel storage tanks for the expanding USAF airbase at Bentwaters in Suffolk.

In spring 1976, Adrian was transferred to the Thames Barrier as part of the new team being formed to be eventually led by John Grice. John arrived six months later, and Adrian soon realised he was working with a very complex and intelligent man, who was going to do things very differently. He respected and valued John's opinions, and how he established relationships with key people. When Warren Hibbs took over the marine works, it became a very effective senior management team.

There were many new staff being recruited to achieve the accelerated programme. Adrian set tough targets, but he was there to listen and support, and determined to get the results. He represented a new breed of younger, intelligent, well-trained managers with an enlightened eighties' management style. He was an excellent role model, got the best from his staff, and was a pleasure to work with.

He was involved with John Grice in the difficult negotiations with the unions in 1978 to get a supplemental agreement approved. Once agreed, all management and the works committee signed up to it, and a small, green book was published, which everyone on the site received. This clearly stated the key objectives and key dates that needed to be achieved to get the bonus payments, and an ending to spurious industrial action.

From that point, progress on site accelerated significantly, driven on by the bonus payments incentive. By 1980, John Grice had completed his work and returned to head office, with Adrian taking over as Project Manager. The last, big push to the final key dates was successfully achieved by completing the outstanding works on the piers, removing all the temporary works and getting the bedding protection completed within two years. This was not easy when there were so many other contractors trying to get access and finish their works at the same time. Adrian achieved all the key dates, and was praised by RPT for the smooth handover and hitting all the targets.

By the end of 1982, Adrian's work was done and he was transferred to Costain International, in Woking, first as Area Manager, then a Director, but he did get back for the opening of the barrier in 1984.

From 1986 to 1992 he was promoted to Managing Director of Costain Civil Engineering, and then became Chairman. It is a precarious life at the top, and others thought it was time for a change. Adrian left Costain and joined the HBG Group in Holland, where he spent a very interesting ten years.

He was working for the international arm, Interbeton, looking after mega-contracts in North

America and challenging jobs in the Caribbean. They partnered with some of the biggest contractors in the USA, working on projects including the Boston Harbour submersed tunnel, and major bridges in California, which was recovering from the devastating 1989 San Francisco earthquake. Another interesting challenge necessitated barging all the materials from Florida to build a new jetty on the remote island of Montserrat, which was later decimated by a volcanic eruption in 2012.

HBG then brought Adrian back to the UK to head up Edmund Nuttall, which had been turned round by his mentor, John Grice, who had now retired. Nuttall were a well-known and respected civils contractor, and in five years under Adrian's leadership, he trebled the turnover and profits.

He was recalled to Holland to take a seat on the main board of the Royal BAM Group in the Netherlands for an exciting period when the company was taken over for a short time by Dragados, a major Spanish conglomerate.

After this very successful and fascinating career, Adrian retired in 2009 to live a less stressful life in West Byfleet in Surrey.

In 1977, new pier managers arrived. Andy Hamilton took over from Dick Conway on Pier 8, and Keith Sargeant started on Pier 7, with Girish Baxi on Pier 6. Girish was in his forties, very experienced and one of several excellent Indian engineers who made a valuable contribution to the barrier. Another was

David Amarasekera, who was a very talented and versatile draughtsman.

The excellent memories of Indian engineers always impressed me. They spoke at least three languages, and were tested in arithmetic from an early age - they also had to learn up to their twenty times table at primary school, whilst we in England were only stretched to a mere twelve.

Graham Burgess and Peter Liggins also arrived to bolster planning and technical support. Engineers came thick and fast. Bob Ford arrived to start the planning on Pier 5, and many younger engineers including Pat Rogers, an Oxford engineering graduate, came to work on Pier 8, and start the planning for the sill lowering of span B. Richard Johnson and Bernie Walsh were good additions to Pier 9. Bernie was also an entertaining raconteur. A few years later, he married a beautiful girl whose father was an admiral in the Argentinian navy, and was apologetically placed under house arrest in Buenos Aires when the Falklands War broke out in 1982. I met him later in Hong Kong, planning new underground lines for the Mass Transit Railway. Mike Burnett came to work on the piers, (never happier than on the back of a motorbike) with Ian Ronchetti, Neil Truphet, and the intriguing Jack Jackson.

Ted Lawton was an innovative temporary-works designer, who had graduated from the Army college at Shrivenham, Oxfordshire. Twenty years and two wives later, we worked together again on the Kap Shui Mun bridge in Hong Kong. Gerry Kerr, (our red-haired representative from Glasgow), Mike Fuller, Keith Durham, and Willie Powles, (who ran off to Paris to marry his French girlfriend), Dave Rothband from Manchester, (renowned for his wit and many female 'cousins,' and sadly missed when he died from a brain tumour in his thirties), Mike Fuller, Neil Staniland and Gary Crabtree. Also Mike Toulson, a very competent engineer who rose up the ladder with Costain after he left the barrier.

There was a nervousness by senior management to employ women engineers on the barrier, which was prevalent in the industry at that time. The main concern was the women's safety. RPT had one woman engineer on site, called Annie Silver, who was not allowed to work night shift, and it was rumoured she was chaperoned home from site during the dark winter evenings.

John Grice was also concerned about employing women engineers on site as he thought they could possibly distract the men from a hectic schedule, and, as far as I know, he never interviewed any. One day an application came in for a site engineer which he read as Carl Wilson. John was tied up with union negotiations and asked Adrian Franklin to carry out the interview, which he did. He was impressed by the candidate, with their experience, knowledge, confidence and immediate availability.

The next day John asked how the interview went. Adrian replied that the interview with Carl didn't go well, but the interview with Carol went very well, and she is starting on Monday! Carol Wilson was the first CTHJV site engineer to start on the barrier and trail-blazed the way for more to follow, much to the satisfaction of the personnel department, and although she wasn't allowed to work night shifts, there were never any problems on site.

Carol Wilson was one of the very few female civil engineers on the barrier, despite the efforts of the personnel departments to try to attract more women to work on the project. Carol was in her twenties, had a degree in Civil Engineering and had been working on the initial Channel Tunnel project at Folkestone in Kent. It was shut down in 1975 by the government as part of the cost-cutting measures. (The work was eventually restarted thirteen years later.) Carol worked on Pier 8 and was very competent, popular and a great role model for young female engineers. Sadly, she died in a sailing accident about ten years later.

Shirley Watson was another well-liked engineer, and Barbara Skeeba, a very exuberant and clever Polish graduate, arrived later with a first class engineering degree from Cambridge University, and worked on the north side for a short time.

The first woman to become a UK chartered civil engineer was Dorothy Buchanan in 1927. She was Scottish, graduated at Edinburgh University, and travelled to London, where she joined Freeman, Fox and Partners. She first worked on the design of the Tyne Bridge in Newcastle, which opened in 1928, then the Sydney Harbour Bridge, Lambeth Bridge, and other projects in Sudan and Northern Ireland. She had a long and successful career and died in 1985. She was quoted as saying,

'I felt that I represented all the women in the world. It was my hope that I would be followed by many others.'

It was not until 2008 that Professor Jean Venables was elected the first woman President of the Institution of Civil Engineers. She was awarded a CBE for her services to the ICE, and has been an inspirational role model for women engineers. But even today, less than 15% of members are women, despite an enormous widening of scope and opportunities over recent years. Jean became a specialist in flood risk management and is

Chair of the Thames Estuary Partnership, and has always had an interest in the Thames Barrier, and its successor.

Another popular engineer working on Pier 9 at this time was Vladimir Vaclavik, (always known as 'Flash') from Lancashire. He was in his forties, of Czech origin, as thin as a rake, with a heavily-lined face that hid many a story, a constant smile and boundless nervous energy. He was very hands on, running from morning to night to sort out problems and help the younger engineers. He did however have a low beer threshold…

On one disturbing occasion he went missing for twenty-four hours triggering a search. After a particularly exuberant celebratory party in the Barrier Arms, Flash was a little the worse for wear, and I was appointed to take him home, (before drink-driving rules came in). He lived about twenty miles away in west Kent, an area I did not know, and I relied entirely on Flash's occasional directions. About an hour later, we arrived in a road he assured me was his. I dropped him off, and he meandered confidently up the drive, and I left him wrestling with his keys.

At 8:00 the next morning we had an important weekly progress meeting, but there was no sign of Flash. Usually he was very conscientious at attending these meetings, and as I was the last to see him, was sternly rebuked by the construction manager and told to find him. At midday and with still no sign of him, his irate wife demanded what we, or rather I, had done with him. I confirmed I had dropped him off where I was directed, and with her eyes cast to heaven, his anxious wife started ringing around the local hospitals and alerted the police. At four o'clock that afternoon, Flash finally made contact, sheepishly confessing that after I had dropped him off, he had somehow mistakenly entered his neighbour's house, fallen asleep on their sofa, and had only just woken up, confused and bewildered. The emergency services were stood down, and I was never asked to chauffer again.

More temporary works designers arrived, including the highly experienced and popular Wally Bradbury, (who sadly, despite being an excellent squash player, died on court at just fifty years old), and the affable Charlie Morley, a very good formwork designer. He was in his fifties, a confirmed bachelor, and delightfully eccentric. He would hold court in the corner of the bar, contently sipping port, with an expression indicating he had just been told a very good joke.

There were many new faces on the commercial side run by the very hard-working David Jenkins and Fred Day. They had bolstered up the team of quantity surveyors, including Lesley Perry and Peter Wilson, (with whom I worked again in Nigeria in 1986) to deal with a mountain of paperwork required by the client for the constant auditing of costs, and for claims submissions.

The procurement department was also extremely busy. My contact was Ernie Hickling, who was always surrounded by huge, clipped sheaves of paper. He was a veteran of many campaigns, with dyed black hair and of indeterminate age. He never appeared to get flustered, and disappeared through the Blackwall Tunnel every night to his family home in Essex. A hard-working engineer, Ian Haining, dealt with the technical queries from the suppliers and was a pleasure to work with, undaunted by the size of the job, and did his best to satisfy panicking engineers getting last-minute orders to site.

THE SUPERVISORS

The engineers could get nothing done without the assistance of the superintendents and the foremen. The size of this site required a senior superintendent to deal with the trade union leaders and emergencies, and be a close adviser to the project manager. This was Stan Kabfell's job.

Stan had been with Costain nearly thirty years and had extensive experience both in the UK and Nigeria. He was a Londoner, a short, stout man in his fifties, clean-shaven except for a fine set of sideburns, and exuded experience and authority. He had a ready smile and keen sense of humour, and managed to get the best out of people in times of adversity. He was on the barrier for almost five and a half years, and gave strong support to the training of young craftsmen in the company. In 1982, he was awarded the British Empire Medal and proudly received it from the Lord-Lieutenant of Greater London, the Right Honourable Baroness Philipps at a ceremony held in London.

Stan's eyes and ears on the site was the general foreman, and when Adrian was appointed, he brought in Gary Bamber, Ken Hodge and other supervisors from Plymouth. Gary was a weary-looking, blond-bearded Yorkshireman who had run his own smaller sites before the barrier. He was in his prime, in his late forties, with plenty of energy to pound the jetties every day, listening to problems, solving disputes before they got out of hand, and above all, keeping everything moving. It was an exhausting job and to assist him was his right-hand man, Terry Parrot, who covered the night shift.

As over 10,000 tonnes of reinforcement steel was required for the concrete in the piers and sills, it was decided to set up steel yards on both sides, and cut and bend the steel on site. On smaller sites it was more economical to get the supplier to cut and bend it at the factory.

Two experienced steelfixing foremen set up a production yard on each side, with powerful cutters that could slice through 40mm-diameter steel bars with ease. Gangs of steel fixers formed production lines, cutting, bending, tagging and loading. It was tough, skilled manual work, which required the steel bars to be bent to within a few millimetres tolerance, or it would give the carpenters problems fixing the formwork. Most of the men were from London, often from families of steel fixers, and the Cockney banter between them would be fierce and very entertaining, keeping their spirits up on a cold winter's day.

Scaffolding was required across the site, and the unenviable scaffolding supervisor in charge was John Haines. He was a tall, popular figure in his forties, who came from north London. Every morning he would liaise with the pier foremen to deal with the daily requirements. The scaffolders needed to be well-trained and fit. Their expertise was essential for keeping everyone safe when moving about the site.

Ken Maybourne was the senior welding supervisor, supplying welders to an unrelenting demand from all over the site. Ken was another Londoner in his forties, always harassed, and running around the site under the watchful eye of the union representatives. It wasn't by coincidence that the welders were the most highly-paid skilled workers on site, after the watermen.

The Pier 9 senior foreman was Arthur Gusterson, a very experienced, affable, grey-haired Shetlander in his late fifties, permanently attached to a cigarette. He was a highly respected man who I never saw panic, having survived coming under heavy fire during World War II. Each day he was there to direct the operatives, carpenters, steel fixers, and to call in welders, scaffolders, electricians, and any other tradesmen that were required that day.

His right-hand man was Eddie Lancaster, a bubbly south-Londoner who had trained as a carpenter. He was a small man, engulfed in a large donkey jacket (covering all the layers), had a large pair of glasses, and was rarely seen without a bobble hat, on which balanced his safety helmet. He was noisy, energetic, and could keep the chippies (carpenters) going. Ken Hodge was the popular Pier 8 foreman from Devon, and had a hypnotising, south-west drawl with a dry sense of humour.

WORKFORCE

In the seventies, most of the workforce were directly employed by the main contractor. They were hired when the contract was won, and laid off when it finished. A radical change began in the eighties; new-style contracts came in, and the main contractors expanded the management role and reduced their site staff and labour to a minimum. Specialist sub-contractors then supplied the labour. This process continues to the present day.

At the beginning of the contract, the majority of the workforce on the barrier came from London or the south-east, with a minority coming from all over the UK. When the site went onto three shifts, there was a deliberate policy to bring more labour from areas with high unemployment - Scotland, the North-East, the Midlands, rural areas of Britain and Ireland.

Many men came from Ireland, as the country was suffering from a chronic lack of work and high unemployment. The ferries were full of young men, keen to work in England, many heading for north-west London around Kilburn to find their contacts. They lived in squalid digs, suffering insults and prejudice, leading many to drink away their sorrows in the evening, missing their families back home. Some married in England, and made enough money by working hard on the building sites to start a fresh life away from London, and prospered.

The Emerald Isle voted to join the European Union in 1973, and the Celtic Tiger started stirring. By the eighties, the ferries were full of Irishmen returning home from England to join the many new projects about to start there. They went home and never returned, and were replaced by a new wave of skilled immigrants from Eastern Europe and Asia.

On site, there were around 500 CTHJV staff and a labour force of over 2000 at the peak, which required another small army of hospitality workers to feed and water them, and maintain and clean washing and toilet facilities. The catering contract was let to Taylor Plan, who provided the temporary kitchens and dining areas in large portacabins, and prepared up to 1900 meals in a twenty-four-hour period.

After three shifts were introduced, the first break was early in each shift. Early mornings were the busiest, when they would make up to 500 breakfasts in ten minutes, with a mountain of sausages and egg-and-bacon sandwiches. The manager was a short, energetic, colourful Italian lady, who kept her team going noisily, and very effectively, in Anglo-Italian. The following summer, she brought her vivacious, seventeen-year old daughter over to gain work experience in the canteen, whose presence caused much interest among the younger workers, and distress for her mother. She ran around like a demented mother hen, shouting at and shooing away any potential suitors in an attempt to save her daughter's honour. The rumour was that she was not successful.

JOHN ANTHONY

There were several 'teaboys,' (as they were called then) on site, men who were coming to the end of their working lives and heading towards their pension. In the dry section office, we had John Anthony, who we all knew as Old John. He was an amiable, good-hearted soul from County Cork with a lovely Irish lilt, who shuffled his way round the office doing his chores, muttering quietly to himself. He would make any refreshments required for meetings, keep the offices clean, and run errands for the senior managers.

One day, John was cleaning Adrian's office and after a few minutes watching the old man wearily sweep the floor, Adrian said to him that he felt embarrassed that an older man was looking after him. John's answer surprised him when he replied,

'You shouldn't be, as there is dignity in all labour.'

Adrian was intrigued at such a profound reply and asked him what he did as a younger man. This was his story.

John Anthony was born and brought up in Cork, and worked for many years for the leading newspaper in Cork, proudly rising up to the rank of senior compositor. He never married, probably as drink and gambling were his weakness, and eventually his downfall, when at around the age of forty, he lost his job. He was devastated and ashamed. He felt he had disgraced his family, and left them and Cork immediately, disappearing without trace. He made no contact with his family from that day.

When he worked on the barrier in 1976, he lived in modest lodgings in Blackheath, and walked to the site every day. One winter morning, he did not turn up for work, which had never happened before. A few hours later, the local police came to the site, and reported that while John was on his way to work, he had been tragically killed by a speeding car on a zebra crossing in Charlton, and had died instantly. A further surprise, but not entirely unexpected, was that John wasn't sixty-five years old, as he had stated, but at least ten years older.

A few weeks later, Adrian went to the funeral to pay his respects, as he felt there would not be many attending, apart from a few friends. He was surprised to see a good turn out, but had to do a double-take when he looked across the room and thought he saw Old John in a dress! One of the other tea boys called Michael noticed Adrian's confusion, and introduced him to the lady who turned out to be John's identical twin! The police in Greenwich had found John's wallet, with an address and photograph in Cork, and had contacted the family.

His sister was understandably sad, but also delighted they had found John after all these years, and that she was able to pay her respects. Adrian was introduced as the top man on the barrier, and she was very impressed that Adrian had come to the funeral for her brother. She asked if John had been happy on the barrier. Adrian confirmed that he had led a very contented life, and that he was well-liked by many. The sister was delighted that she could return to Cork and share this news with the family. They had presumed all sorts of things since he left Ireland, but they now knew that he had pulled back from the brink, and had led a good and meaningful life.

Adrian reflected how sad it was, that John had been so ashamed that he had purposely estranged himself from those he loved, and who loved him. A noble act, but so sad that he had felt unable to return to his family, particularly as he had kept a little clipping in his wallet as a reminder of his previous life.

ACCOMODATION

A large number of staff lived away from their homes and returned at weekends, so the local hotels, bedsits and boarding houses in the area did very well out of the barrier over the next five years.

A frequently used hotel was The Clarendon, a Georgian hotel owned by the O'Donnell family, sited on the edge of Blackheath village. It was a Grade II listed, four-storey building, part of an imposing terrace, with an excellent view overlooking the historic heath and a five-minute walk from Greenwich Park. From here you could see London stretch out to the horizon, with the River Thames winding its way through the many areas the barrier was being built to protect.

Many historic events had occurred on Blackheath, from Wat Tyler's disastrous uprising - The Peasant's Revolt, a motley band of men who bravely marched from Kent and were slaughtered on the heath in 1381, to Henry V being greeted on his return from France by cheering crowds, all dressed in red, after his astounding victory at the Battle of Agincourt in 1415. Then there was the bubonic plague, (better known as the Great Plague) in 1664-66, when thousands of bodies were brought from London and buried in deep pits on the heath.

A few of the senior managers were resident at The Clarendon, some staying for several years, not good for their health or marriages, but it was very convenient for meetings and dining with clients, with a decent restaurant and bar. Some of the antics that occurred in The Clarendon over these years became enshrined in Blackheath's history, no doubt embellished at each re-telling.

One particular story involved a senior commercial manager who had been celebrating after a particularly stressful but successful day, and was a little worse for wear whilst trying to find his room. After several attempts trying to enter various rooms, on different floors, he eventually found the correct one, and after entering his room, threw off all his clothes and collapsed on the bed. Waking a short time later, desperately in need of the facilities, he stumbled into what he thought was the bathroom. It was not. He had gone out of his room, into the corridor, and the door had closed behind him. Confused and bewildered, he wandered off and relieved himself in an ornate and convenient plant pot before settling down to sleep. The following morning, a member of staff had a call from an agitated female guest asking for help. She had found him fast asleep on the carpet of the corridor of the floor below his room, stark naked. They gently woke him, and led him discretely back to his room. He stayed on at the hotel for another two years.

For the travelling workforce, CTHJV also offered less salubrious, and much cheaper alternative accommodation at a caravan site in Thamesmead, amongst a new development a few miles from the site.

The Thamesmead development was built by the GLC in the 1960s as a showcase, to take families from overcrowded Victorian slums in south-east inner London. The area had been inundated by the Great Flood of 1953, when the surge water poured over the inadequate flood defences. In case the new flood defences were not in place before the next surge, the architects designed living accommodation at first-floor level or above, with connecting overhead walkways, and leaving the ground floors as garage space. In 1968 the first phase was completed with a variety of modernist town houses and concrete, twelve-storey high-rise blocks, which were popular with planners at that time. It was a disaster. The unattractive concrete jungle had walkways that were quickly covered in graffiti and became crime havens at night. The occupants were prisoners in their own flats, with frequent outbreaks of criminality, and social and health problems. Several films were made in Thamesmead, set in this so-called Utopia, including *A Clockwork Orange* directed by Stanley Kubrick.

I visited the caravan site once. For young, lowly-paid engineers and travelling men it was adequate but very basic, and not for those of a nervous disposition. The young engineer I was visiting had recently graduated from Cambridge. He was highly intelligent, but eccentric, and recovering from the recent death of his brother. His father had been a missionary in Africa in the 1960s and he had been quite used to sleeping on a mud floor in simple huts, and eating frugally. As a result he found his lowly caravan most adequate. He also had a love of barges, and was building one behind his caravan. Somehow, he had acquired a large metal hull, (unloaded with the help of the plant department), and was in the process of welding it together. He was an early eco-warrior, and I often wondered in which direction he would go after he left the barrier.

All these many hundreds of new faces brought fresh stimulus to the small businesses of Charlton and Woolwich. They boomed over the next five years, and the area revived and thrived after we had all moved on, ready for the massive redevelopment of Docklands.

6

1977 – PART 2

DEWATERING

The dewatering of the Pier 9 cofferdam was carried out slowly, in several stages, starting in December 1976 and completed in January 1977. This was to allow the effectiveness of the pressure relief system to be checked, and to ensure there were no problems with the internal strutting of the cofferdam, which was being revealed for the first time.

The first problem encountered was a significant volume of water gushing through some of the clutches of the sheet piles that had split during piling. As they were temporary works, they were partially sealed with sawdust and ashes, or plated where necessary. This was a time consuming business, and the design and commercial teams were immediately assigned to look at the option of heavier piles for the north cofferdams.

Once dewatered, the surface of the underwater concrete was removed, the pumps checked, lighting installed, and temporary access stairs erected by the scaffolders. Now we could walk down twelve metres below the river bed to the base of the pier for the first time. Water poured down the inside of the piles, and spray created small rainbows when the sun caught it. You could feel the deep throbbing of the engines of passing ships, and the heavy vibration of large pumps and generators on the access jetties. Add to this a gaggle of concrete breakers pecking away at the surface of the concrete to remove the laitance and to form a simple drainage system, and it looked like a scene from one of the *Alien* movies. Those who stood on the top of the underwater concrete before construction started were made members of the select 'Pier 9 Bottomers Club'.

SURVEYORS

Once access was possible, the surveyors came from their office on site to set up the key stations. They were overseen by a senior surveying manager who ran teams of eager young surveyors, assistants and carriers, (then called chainmen, harking back to a time when distances were measured with metal chains), who were dispatched to every corner

The teams carried large boxes of equipment, often on their backs, and due to long hours of standing, needed a multitude of layers of clothing to keep warm, usually mud-splattered and damp. Engulfed in clouds of cigarette smoke, they had the appearance of bands of itinerant travellers, and were a surprisingly cheerful bunch. Their role was crucial. They could afford no mistakes, with all their calculations meticulously checked by the senior surveyors. In the 1970s, GPS was still in early development, and the majority of surveys were done using theodolites, with calculations carried out on steam-driven calculators or by slide rule. It was very tedious compared with the lightning-quick speed of modern technology. The reward was the satisfaction of seeing the jigsaw come together before their eyes and fit perfectly, due to meticulous care and attention to detail.

The primary control points for all the surveying on the barrier were two stations, sited each side of the River Thames. These provided a base-line around 560 metres apart from which all the piers would be set out. Twelve-metre-high towers were erected over each station to ensure a clean line of sight across the river during the construction of all the piers, and the base-line was referenced to several established trigonometrical stations on the land. As each pier was dewatered and the top of the concrete prepared, another twelve-metre-high tower would be erected in the middle of each pier. A laser plummet was used to transfer the point on the tower down onto the concrete, and four setting-out points were established, one at each end, and two in the centre. The east-west centre-line could then be established by turning a right angle with a theodolite, and all the setting out of the pier could be done from these points. Constant checking was essential to ensure there had been no movement of the structure, critical for the when the gates and machinery were installed.

CONCRETE

Early in 1974, CTHJV had identified that there was going to be difficulty with the specification that RPT had requested for the many mass concrete pours. Their concern was how to limit the amount of thermal cracking that would occur when pouring large volumes of concrete. To overcome this, they limited the height of the pour, and wanted to use two different mixes, one for the outer and another for the inner areas, based on experience on a large mass concrete dam in the West Country.

CTHJV spent a lot of time looking at the practicalities of doing this, and decided there were far too many risks involved, and would offer an alternative of a single unified mix. The Concrete Societies in both the UK and USA were approached and made some very helpful suggestions. After further discussions with the concrete manager, Clive Carden, he began supervising the testing of many mixes in the laboratory. Eventually, an acceptable unified mix was found and submitted to RPT. Long discussions and more testing ensued, as any correction later would have been extremely costly in both money and time. A mix was eventually accepted in 1975, and was used for the first time on Pier 9 in 1976, with temperature measurements made at every conceivable point. It passed with flying colours.

THE STRIKE

It was a strange feeling when the workers downed tools at the end of May, and the site fell eerily silent. A picket line was set up by the unions at the main gates, with the usual banners and noisy chants, but as the strike drifted into summer, enthusiasm waned, and the occasional deck chair was spotted at the gates. The engineering and commercial staff continued to work, and we walked or drove through the picket lines to a generally good-humoured barrage of insults. There was a slight feeling of relief by the engineers; pressures had been building up to complete the preparations for the new shifts, and this was a chance to get further forward planning done.

Methods were fine-tuned and improved, work schedules

prepared, materials ordered and brain storming meetings held. It was a productive time, and we were able to get ahead for the first time. The workshops did not remain quiet for long either, with some of the foremen honing their carpentry skills in their breaks, producing some excellent pieces of furniture. One of the engineers used his lunchtimes to completely renovate an old, sad-looking E-Type Jaguar with a deteriorating white body and the remains of red upholstery. He did an excellent job, and on completion two months later, was cheered loudly as he proudly drove the gleaming vehicle out slowly through the picket line.

At the beginning of July, the exhausted negotiators finally reached an agreement with the unions on the implementation of three eight-hour shifts, and work resumed.

SILVER JUBILEE

1977 was the Silver Jubilee year of HM Queen Elizabeth II. One of the celebrations was held on July 9, when a pageant of barges travelled up the River Thames from Greenwich to Westminster Bridge to salute Her Majesty.

The Joint Venture directors decided the barrier should enter a decorated barge, which would boost morale on site and get some much-needed positive publicity after the strike. It was decided to adopt the theme of King Canute holding back the tide. The watermen, led by Frankie Barratt, found an appropriate vessel, and set up scaffolding inside the barge to lay out a plywood platform. This was then covered with some lurid-green artificial grass.

An impressive throne was built at the front of the barge with the Canute figure holding out his polystyrene hands defiantly. Someone representing Britannia would sit proudly next to him. Jill Brock, one of the typists, who had the look of a valiant warrior queen, volunteered enthusiastically for this role. She bravely chose a flowing, white dress with a red sash and a suitable helmet, and the welders provided her with a disturbingly large trident and shield. A raffle was held to choose the thirty people to go on board, and I was one of the lucky ones.

There were eighteen men and twelve women, including three Dutchmen - Bert Lugtenberg, Elbert Van De Berg and Willem Prins, with two crew to steer the barge, which had a motor attached at the back. Peter Blaseby, a senior planning engineer, was appointed to organise it, and he set about his task with great zeal. Everyone was to dress in white jeans and a white tee-shirt with the Thames Barrier Project logo emblazoned in a gaudy, red, felt-like material on the front. Peter was a keen rower and got permission for the barge to be moored at the jetty of his club, the Greenwich Curlew Rowing Club, where we could all board.

On July 9 we arrived at the rowing club at five in the afternoon for a quick drink and boarded refreshed an hour later, struggling up the gangway with enough boxes of alcohol to last us the evening. We soon found our sea-legs and some got into the party mood very quickly, including Britannia.

The SS *Barrier* cast off, and we joined the impressive procession of at least fifty assorted vessels decked out in a wide variety of themes. They were spread out right across the Thames in a long line, decorated with bunting, flags and banners, forming a colourful procession. There was a buzz of excited conversation from our motley crew and raucous laughter drifting across the river as we set off, a scene Old Father Thames must have witnessed many times over the centuries.

The barge adjacent to us was from a large brewery, and their theme was, not surprisingly, a square-shaped public bar, with working taps and a row of optics, with revellers sitting on all four sides.

All was well for the first ten minutes, and then a light drizzle started, turning into a steady, warm, soaking Irish rain, which continued unrelentingly for the next three hours.

In the first hour, we passed the depressing sight of many closed and derelict warehouses, abandoned wharfs and decaying docks around Bermondsey, waiting to be developed. However, it was encouraging to see the lights on in the *Prospect of Whitby*, which was built in 1520 and is the oldest riverside tavern in England. I looked across at the brewery barge, where the revellers had mysteriously disappeared, maybe into a comfy snug-bar below deck, which gave it the appearance of a ghostly *Marie Celeste*.

After two hours in the rain, we rounded the final bend of the river to see in the distance the distinctive tower of the Oxo building, which signalled we were approaching Tower Bridge. The bridge was packed with enthusiastic crowds cheering and waving to the flotilla of barges, and enjoying every minute of the nautical spectacle, even in the pouring rain.

By this time, the artificial grass on our boat had become a lethal skid pan, with many slightly inebriated mariners struggling to keep upright, and ending up with green skid marks down their back. Luckily there were no injuries, with plenty of handrails and lifebelts to hang on to. The bright red dye from the lettering had trickled down the front of the tee-shirts and we looked like a bunch of blood-stained zombies in a scene worthy of a Hammer horror film. This though was forgotten as the cheers of the crowds got louder and echoed as we passed under each historic bridge, slowly meandering our way upriver towards Westminster Bridge.

Britannia had her own problems. Perched precariously on her throne, she had been calming her soaked nerves with a bottle of white plonk, and needed to reach forward to steady herself as a mighty bow-wave approached. Conveniently, Canute's hand was beckoning, but within seconds, three fingers snapped off in Britannia's grasp, leaving only one middle finger sticking defiantly in the air. As there was no way of re-attaching the fingers, this unfortunately was what Her Majesty may have spotted through the Irish mist that night, as she stood on the balcony of County Hall near Westminster Bridge. It would certainly have entertained the Duke of Edinburgh, who was standing beside her.

It was late by the time the tired, disheveled and very happy crew disembarked back at Greenwich, with the evening deemed a resounding success, and an unforgettable barrier experience.

SOUTH SIDE PROGRESS

Once we were back to work, it took a few weeks to get the new labour and staff supervision in place. I was working shifts on Pier 9 as the structure started to rise from the depths. In August, I also worked on the Pier 7 underwater concrete pour, the last to be completed on the southern piers. It was also the biggest to date at 6400m3, but this no longer daunted us. It was now becoming a well-oiled operation, with all aspects of the pour going smoother and faster. By the time Pier 3 was ready, the final on the north side in 1980, we had almost doubled the hourly rate, and had created a world record for underwater concrete poured.

Pier 7 dewatering started in November 1977, after the final two bracings were fixed. The dewatering went smoothly, but within a few days, a fine crack appeared across the top of the concrete, and was getting bigger. The readings of the installed pressure relief wells were rising significantly, indicating that the sheet pile cut-off wall was not working. Divers were sent down to investigate, and they found significant river bed erosion on the outside of the sheet piles of the cofferdam.

We knew that the geology under Pier 7 was the most complex of all the piers. There were several minor fault lines in the chalk in the middle of the Thames that had been picked up by bore-holes in the initial site investigations in 1972. Pier 7 was sitting on one of them. There was evidence of heavy fissuring in the chalk around the fault line and this was the problem.

A ground works expert, Professor Stuart Littlejohn, was immediately called in from one of the London universities to carry out an examination and submit a report to the consultants. He recommended the cofferdam be refilled, and to use a specialist sub-contractor to install a 40m-long grout curtain on either side of the cofferdam. Colcrete was the sub-contractor, and it took two months to complete the grouting. That cured the problem, and the water pressure started to drop. RPT carried out further checks and they gave the all-clear to continue. The cofferdam was cautiously and successfully dewatered in April 1978, but we had lost four months on the programme.

SHIFTWORK

During the strike, the plans for the three-shift, twenty-four-hour working, were developed, discussed and agreed with the unions. The three shifts were 08:00 to 16:00, 16:00 to midnight, and midnight to 08:00, with a thirty minutes hand-over allowed at the end of each shift. The shifts were rotated weekly, and I personally found this very draining. There just wasn't enough time for the body clock to adjust when the work hours were being changed every week, and many of us felt permanently tired after a very short time.

This was very risky on a building site, where a momentary lack of concentration in many areas could easily cost lives. I heard the decision to use weekly rotations was probably based on factory data, not the best choice for a construction site. It would have been more productive to have implemented monthly rotations. Luckily, we saw no increase in accidents during this period.

Once the cofferdam was dry and access secured, the survey-ors were the next down into the cofferdam, getting their control points in. From these points the engineers would set out the positions of the formwork. Once the consultants had completed their checks on the surface of the underwater concrete, the first reinforcement was lowered down onto the concrete, and the steelfixers started laying out and fixing steel for the first part of the permanent structure.

They would be followed closely by the carpenters, who would fix the vertical form-work supported by an array of propping systems. The first five levels, still three metres below the river bed level, were in a rectangular shape, which incorporated the sumps under the sills. They would house the sill jacking systems, and start forming the profile of the sill itself. With only a few millimetres tolerance, much checking and double-checking went on at these critical levels to ensure they were right. It would be too late when the sills were being lowered.

The carpenters shop and the steelyard had been working to full capacity before the underwater concrete pours. This would ensure the formwork and the steel reinforcement would be ready for the first lifts as soon as the pier was dewatered. By this time, the large steelyards on the north and south sides were a hive of activity, with teams of men cutting and bending the reinforcement bars, from schedules fed through from engineers on the various piers. The piers were to be built in mostly 1.5m-high lifts, with each numbered, and all the shutters and steel schedules of that lift given the same number. These numbers were critical, as the stockyards were now full, and in a tired moment, it would be easy to choose the wrong one. Every day there was a continuous stream of trailers feeding materials to the piers, as construction of the concrete piers finally got under way on the south side.

NORTH SIDE DRAMAS

Meanwhile, on the north side, the construction of the first four sills in the dry dock was going well, with the massive, concrete structures which loomed over the workers quickly taking shape.

The first subway liners were about to be installed in the sills, having been sub-contracted to Alfred Allen in their fabrication shop in the Midlands. The first stage was to manufacture the liners into 10-metre sections at the works, and transport them to site. Three of these sections were then welded together on a production line adjacent to the sill, and lifted into place by two cranes in tandem. Once again, there was only a few millimetres tolerance to enable the line-up with the bellow units flanges in the piers, and internal strutting, and a high standard of welding was essential to ensure roundness for the final weld. It was essential the shrinkage of the butt welds were closely controlled to ensure the result matched the sill's design length. Each stage was closely watched by RPT inspectors, and it was a success. A further tribute to British workmanship.

The scallops were being formed and also required fine tolerances, so were all finished by hand and checked again when finished. It was essential there were no problems when the gates were fitted.

The foundations of Pier 2 and the north abutment had also started smoothly, using the experiences gained on the south side. The works on the north side had advanced to such an extent they had to slow down a little to let the south piers catch up. It was about this time that I understand, a sharp-eyed junior quantity surveyor, who had come into work on a Bank Holiday morning to finish some urgent work, spotted a 40-tonne trailer arrive from the steel supplier, carrying a full load of steel reinforcing bars. This was not unusual, but the lorry left shortly after entering the yard without unloading. In 1977, CCTV was predominantly used for monitoring traffic around London, and most security was carried out by staff from security companies patrolling and checking, a tedious job, often poorly paid, and open to criminal offers.

The young quantity surveyor reported these comings and goings to his superior, and he was instructed to observe and follow any other lorries and find out where they were going. Sure enough, the scene was repeated on the following Bank Holiday and several Sundays, and was obviously a well-planned operation. Our very own 'Sherlock' followed the lorries to a yard in Silvertown, where the steel bars were swiftly unloaded and transferred. After further investigation, it became apparent this was a well-organised job that had been going on for some time, and the police were brought in.

They very quickly identified Jimmy Wynn, the steel foreman, as running the operation and he confessed straight away. He was a Scotsman in his forties, popular and very good at his job. Ironically, he had been frequently complimented on how efficiently he had been running the yard. He came from a prosperous family of steelfixers in the east end of London, who were well-known around Bermondsey.

He was charged with conspiracy to steal, an offence more complicated to prove than theft. It also carried a much higher sentence, that CTHJV were eager to see imposed. Each company in the CTHJV consortium instructed their own barristers to represent them, which complicated things. A date was fixed for the hearing, and the trial was to be held at Woolwich Magistrates Court. (The Crown Court was not opened until 1992).

When it came to how much steel was stolen, it became very confusing, as the CTHJV monitoring system had become too complicated – there were no computers or spreadsheets. All records were kept manually and the gang left few paper traces. As the scam had been going on for over a year, it would have involved the theft of hundreds of tons of reinforcement steel. The legal arguments dragged on for months, with the defence counsel concentrating on the weakness of the CTHJV material control system on the site, and the difficulty the poor foreman had in using it!

The judge decided to visit the site with the barristers, the jury and Jimmy. I was there on that sunny day, and watched the crocodile line weave its way by coach through the site. When Jimmy arrived at the steelfixers yard, a huge cheer went up from his fellow workers, much to the annoyance of the judge. Each part of the control system was explained to everyone assembled, and an unimpressed jury returned to the court.

The defence counsel took full advantage of what he had seen, and sowed further doubt in the jury's mind. After the final statements, the jury went out for a short deliberation and returned with the verdict of not guilty. In the judge's summing up, he lambasted CTHJV for the complicated material control system that only a few understood, and criticised the police for bringing the wrong charge. The charge of theft would have been straight forward, and not wasted a lot of taxpayer's money.

Jimmy was released, but realising he could still be charged with theft, he fled to Nigeria, after throwing a big farewell party. A year later, he returned homesick, and was eventually re-arrested, and charged. He pleaded guilty and was given a relatively short custodial sentence. The final amount stolen was never known, except possibly by a few select East End families, and probably the underworld. The CTHJV procurement system was given a thorough overhaul.

ig 3. GLC Project Manager Ray Horner, *Father of the Barrier*
ig 4. The Thames Barrier 1982

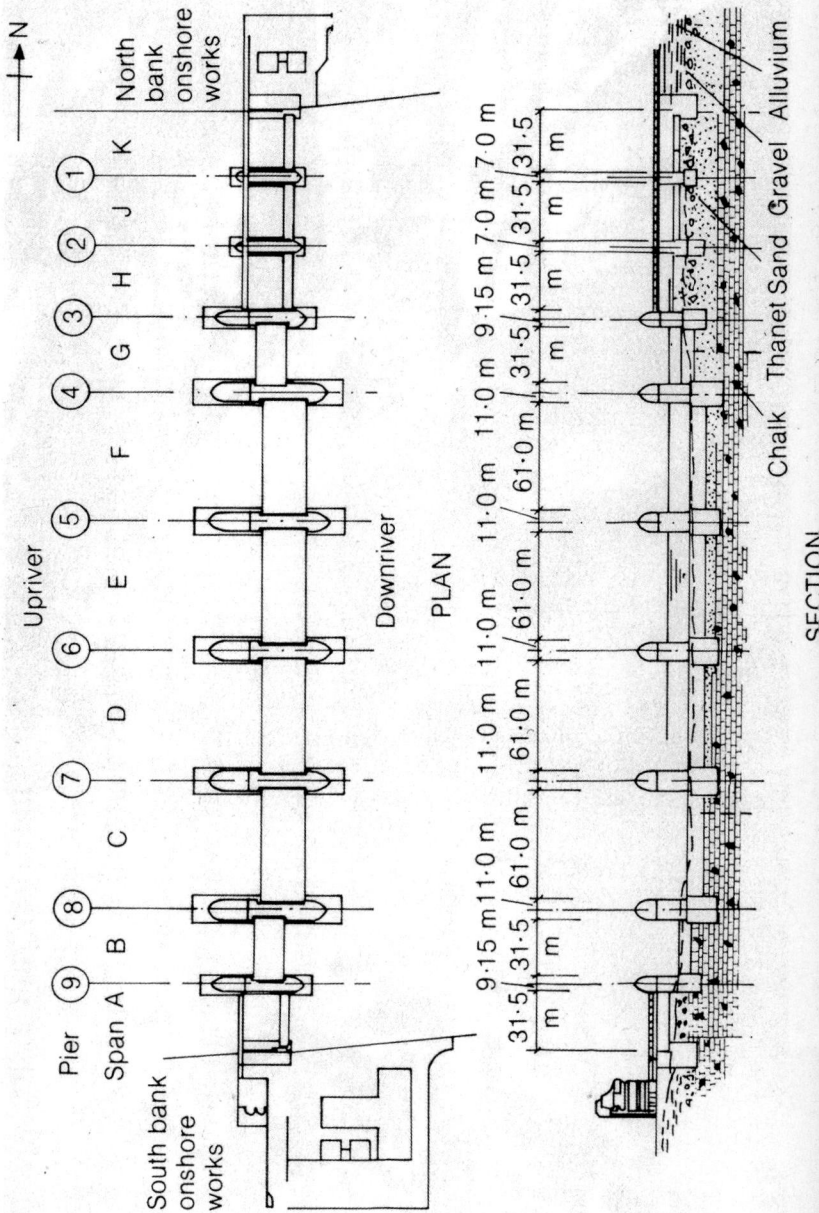

Fig 5. Plan and section of the Thames Barrier

Figs 6-10. *Clockwise from top left:*
Peter Cox, Senior Partner
Alan Mitchell, Chief Engineer for the Civils Design
George Davis, Engineer's Representative on site
John Hounslow, Senior engineer and first Barrier Manager
Charlie Draper, Mechanical Engineer and Inventor

Below:
Fig 11. Rising Sector Gate positions

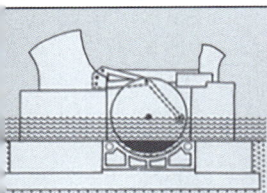

GATE IN NORMAL LOWERED POSITION.

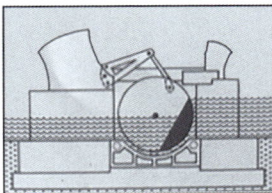

GATE RISING.

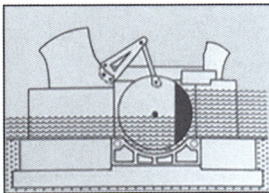

GATE IN FLOOD DEFENCE POSITION.

Figs 12-19. *Clockwise from top left:*
John Reeve, Project Director
John Grice, Project Manager 1977-1980
Adrian Franklin, Project Manager 1980–82
Eric Napier, Deputy Project Manager
Warren Hibbs, Marine Works Manager 1977-1982
Paul Sivey, Construction Manager, North side
Rick Randall, Construction Manager, Sill Sinking
Stan Kabfell, Senior Supervisor and Gary Bamber, Site Senior Supervisor

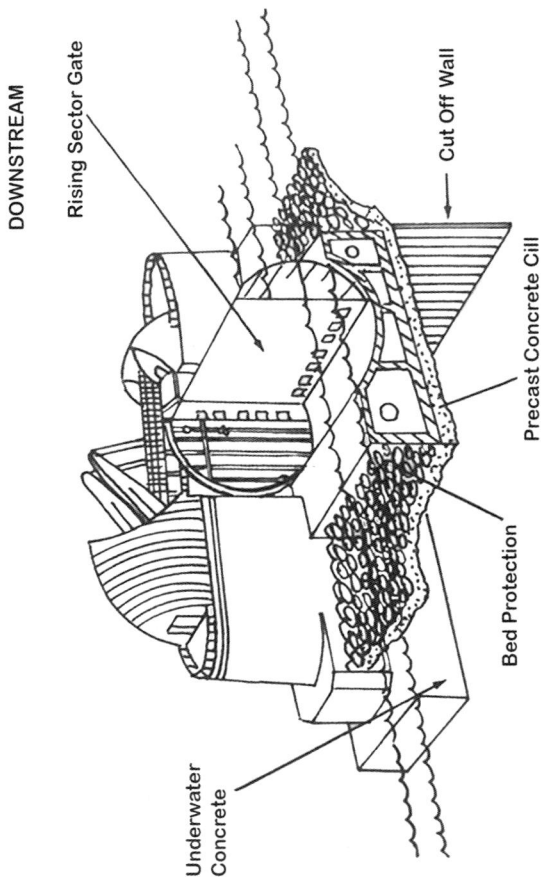

Figs 20-22.
Top left to right:
Fig 20.
Don Langdown,
Chief Engineer
Fig 21.
Aavid Degonaars,
HBM Engineering
Manager
Fig 22.
Peter Blaseby,
Senior Planner

Fig 23. Isometric section of Pier and Sill

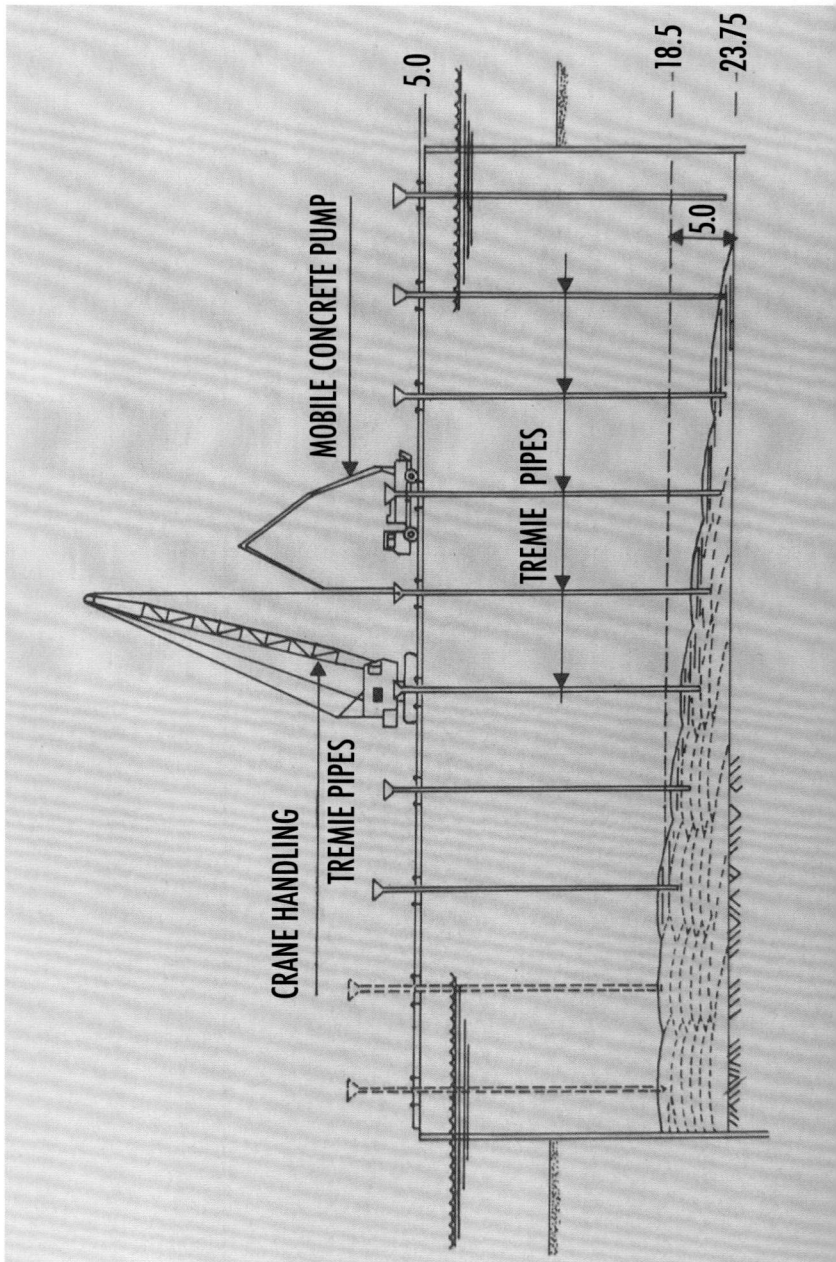

Fig 24. Section showing the placing of underwater concrete

Fig 25. 1976 Piling for Pier 9 and South Abutment

Fig 26. 1976 Completing Cofferdams and Excavation of Piers 6-9

Fig 27. 1976 Preparing for underwater concrete

Fig 28. Clearing laitance on surface of underwater concrete

Fig 29. 1976 Pier 9 construction at lower level

Fig 30. Lifting the Trunnion into Pier 4

Fig 31. 1977 Trunnion in position in Pier 8

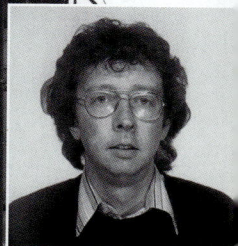

Fig 32. Alistair Handford Manager Pier 3

Fig 33. Adrian Franklin, Girish Baxi, Ray Genoni and others of the Dry Section Team

ig 34. 1977 Phase 1 Sill construction on the north bank

ig 35. 1977 Aerial view of north dry dock

Figs. 36-38. 1977 Silver Jubilee Pageant

Fig. 39. 1977 Thames Barge Race

Fig. 40. Watermen supervisor, Frankie Barrett

Fig 41. 1977 Flooding north dry dock for Sill Tow Out

Fig 42. Sill Tow Out from George V dock

Fig 43. Sill positioning at the pier

Fig 44. Sill lowering, control cabin

Fig 45. Water filling of Sill scallop before lowering

Above:
Fig 46.
Shell roof
construction
at Tysons
1977

Fig 47.
Erecting the
shell roof on
Pier 9 1980

Fig 48. Start of Phase 2 of Sill Construction

Warren Hibbs

Don Langdown

Rick Randall

Peter Blaseby

Chris Gane

Figs. 49-53. 1979 Wobbler Awards

Fig 54. Bill Macey, Project Director

Fig 55. Dick Thorp, Project Manager

Fig 56. Placing the Gate Arm

Fig 57. Positioning the first Gate Leaf

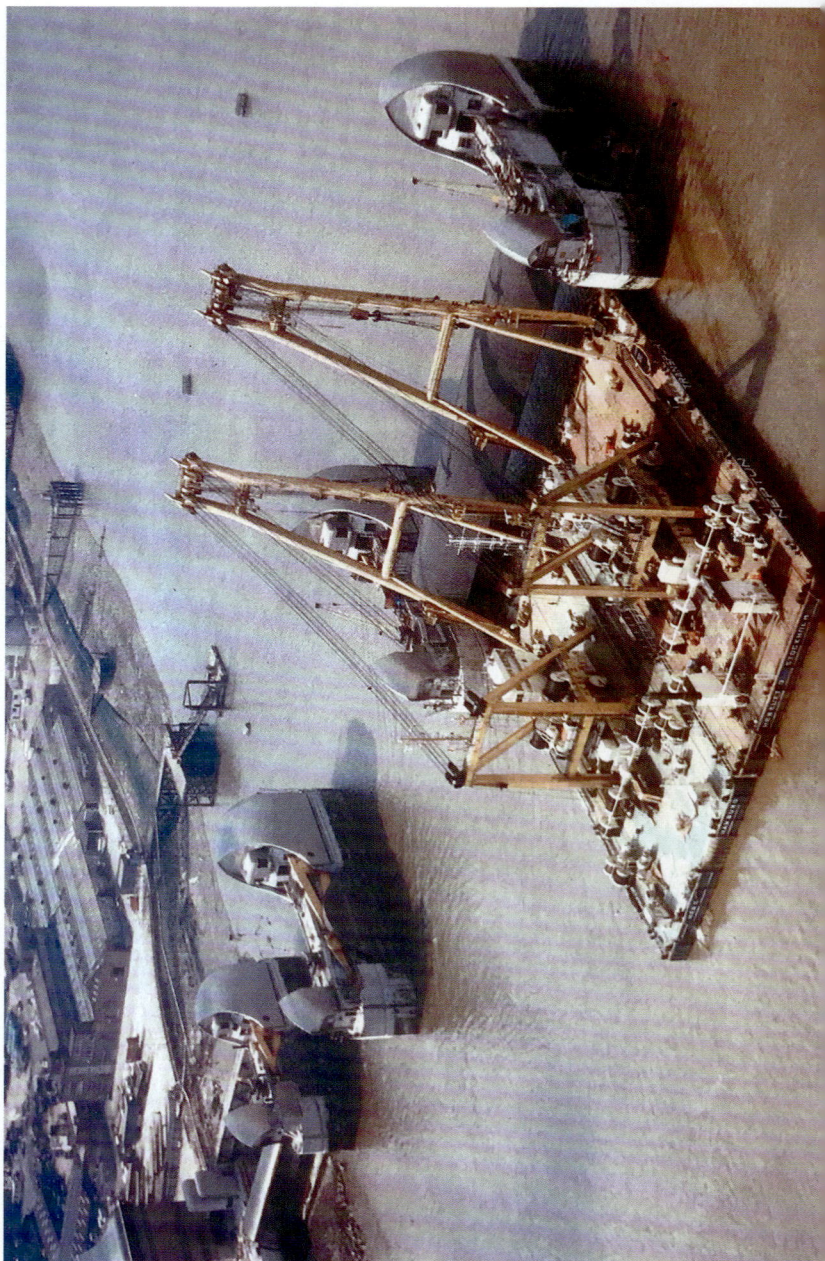

Fig 58. Lowering the first Gate Leaf

Fig 59. Placing Bed
Protection between
Pier 1 and Pier 2

Fig 60. Marine
Engineer
Ken Limburn
supervising rock
protection

Fig 61. Tarmac engineers and supervisors

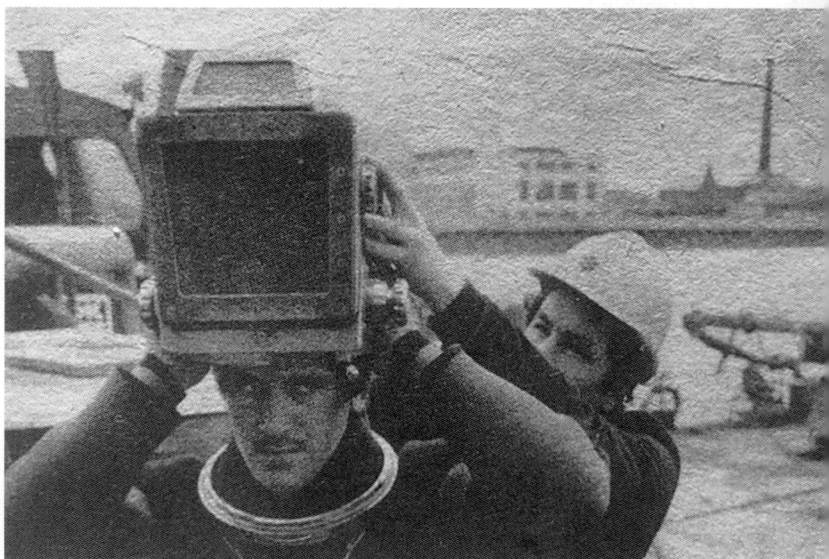

Fig 62. Engineer Bob Alan assisting diver

Fig 63. 1982 Final Testing

Fig 64. Sill cable subway

Fig 65. Control Room testing

Fig 66. Royal Opening Ceremony May 8 1984

Fig 67. RPT Introductions to HM Queen Elizabeth

Fig 68. CTH Introductions to HM Queen Elizabeth

Fig 69. 1992 Anniversary Visit

Fig 70. 1992 Author Rory O'Grady visit

Fig 71. 1984 Thames Barrier completed

Fig 72. HMS Belfast passing through barrier

Fig 73. HMS Ark Royal Passing through barrier

Fig 74. Thames Barrier gates all raised

1977- A RACE ODYSSEY

To help cement the new relationship with the workers on site, the CTHJV board decided to hold a skiff regatta at Greenwich during the summer.

Thames skiffs were developed in the 19th century primarily for leisure, and several clubs survive to this day. Their design was based on the Thames wherries and shallops, which had been operated by the Thames watermen as a water taxi service since Tudor times.

Skiffs have fixed rather than sliding seats, and the blades are held in hole pins at the side of the boats rather than outriggers, and are made of wood. It takes a great deal of skill and stamina to operate them. The boats were loaned by the London Fire Brigade and there was keen interest in the race.

Thirty-two teams entered, representing all the trades on the site, with a crew of four in each boat. After preliminary races, the final four contestants were the scaffolders, the divers, the electricians and the piling hands. The scaffolders took an early lead but it was the divers that came through and won the race, captained by Bill McKean with Tony Martin, John Shaw, and Karl Robinson. To finish a very successful day there was also a race between CTHJV and RPT staff. CTHJV started well but RPT caught up and won by two and a half lengths. Celebrations finished up once more in the Barrier Arms.

BRAVERY AWARD

The year ended with a heartwarming story. One of the workers, Bert Hook, a Londoner, was awarded the Royal Humane

Society's Bronze Medal and certificate for saving a man's life.

Bert had been working as a piling hand on the cofferdams, and was on a nearby safety boat when a 14-tonne steel piling hammer suddenly started operating without warning. It smashed against a steel gate placed on the cofferdam, where five of the piling team were standing. Four of them clung on, but the fifth man was thrown into the water, which was a bitterly cold 8°C. Bert saw the man struggling, his head bobbing in the water. Without hesitation, he threw off his coat and boots, dived into the freezing river, and swam to the man. Bert held onto him until the safety boat drew alongside and helped them into the boat. Without a doubt he saved the man's life.

The award was presented by the Lord Lieutenant of Greater London, Lord Elworthy at a special ceremony at County Hall, with Bert's family proudly looking on.

7

1978

THE GATES

Whilst work had been progressing steadily on site, the manufacture of the gates and operating machinery by the Davy Cleveland Barrier Consortium (DCBC) was well ahead, having started in early 1975.

Due to the enormous size and weight of the gates, they were split into sub-assemblies and these were fabricated at the Cleveland Bridge Darlington works. The final assembly and transportation arrangements were carried out at their Port Clarence yard.

There had been lengthy discussions with the designer (RPT) on the fabrication procedures to ensure built-in residual stresses were kept to a minimum. The plate arrangements and welding methods used were all critical, and the welding was closely watched by RPT inspectors at the yards. The tolerances being applied were more exacting than on many major bridges. The curved surfaces of the gates were fabricated uppermost, which suited both manufacture, where well-established techniques could be used, and handling. The gates are hollow, but they are heavily braced inside with internal diaphragms and cross members, thus better for welding in this position and easier to handle at the works and on site.

The gate arms had to be broken down in a similar manner, with the sub-assemblies also manufactured at the Darlington works.

The Port Clarence yard is located on the banks of the River Tees, about twenty miles away from the Darlington works. Therefore the sub-assemblies had to be transported by road, and could not be more than six metres long, two metres wide, 5.3 metres high and weigh no more than 50 tonnes, to enable them fit onto the transporters. To get all the parts for the gates down to the assembly yard required many trips.

The yard was in an exposed location on the coast, where conditions could be particularly harsh in winter, with minimal cover. There was a wide range of temperatures over the year, or even over a sunny day, and consequently, this could be a headache for those checking the steel dimensions.

In order to guarantee dimensional accuracy, it was essential critical welding of the sub-section units was done at night. This ensured any potential differential temperature distortion of the units was kept to a minimum. Unfortunately, that meant the dimensional checks also had to be done at night, which was not popular with the welders' families.

Once all the welding was complete, the units could go to the paint shop. All exposed surfaces had to be shot-blasted until, *'You could eat your dinner off them'*, (to quote one engineer), before the high-specification coating was applied under strict conditions of temperature and humidity. After final checks, the units were put into storage awaiting their journey to London.

Detailed planning went into the transportation of the sub-assembly of the first gate when it was conveyed from Darlington to Port Clarence, with the widths of the road, street furniture and the bridge clearances all carefully checked. The transporter left on time, but what they hadn't bargained for was driver error. Somehow, he managed to take a wrong turning early in the journey, despite having a police escort. After an hour elapsed, with no sign of this valuable consignment arriving at Port Clarence, a search party was sent out. To their horror, they found the first section of the Thames Barrier gate stuck in the middle of a housing estate, surrounded by a crowd of intrigued onlookers. After much careful manoeuvring, it was slowly eased out of Arcadia Drive and, to the cheers and good-humoured mockery from the crowd, it set off to Port Clarence with no further incident.

The first gate was nearly complete by the end of 1977, but it would be three years before it was loaded onto a multitude of bogies, and rolled onto a sixty-metre-long barge, and towed to the Thames estuary.

The beauty of having four identical main gates soon became apparent. Construction procedures could be repeated, giving considerable saving on total fabrication time. Production continued smoothly. Unfortunately, due to the delays on site, the fabrication had to be slowed down. Luckily, Cleveland Bridge was able to transfer resources off the barrier gates and onto other, more urgent contracts. Cleveland Bridge also had to build additional storage sheds at Port Clarence to protect and ensure no deterioration to the external surfaces of the gates, all of which resulted in considerable additional costs to the client.

OTHER CONTRACTS

Another vital contract was the manufacture of the massive, steel, shaft support structures, (the trunnions), and was let to Voest, the Austrian National Steel Corporation in March 1974.

The trunnions are the fulcrums for the 61m-long gates, and needed to be concreted into the piers at an early stage of construction. They were substantial, hollow, steel cylinders up to three metres in diameter, with bolts at either end, strengthened with circumferential ribs, and weighed up to 125 tonnes.

Shortly after being awarded the contract, Voest ran into financial difficulties, as the pound was going through another crisis, and its value had dropped significantly against the Austrian schilling. They therefore proposed to sub-contract some of the trunnions to the Belgium company, Cockerill-Ougree, based at Liège, to reduce transport costs. RPT inspected and approved the facilities at Liège, and manufacturing proceeded.

The first casting went ahead in August 1974, and the last unit was completed in April 1977. RPT requested that a trial be arranged to demonstrate how the trunnion would be lifted out of a barge on site, and lowered into position on the pier with pinpoint accuracy. The demonstration all went very smoothly.

In late 1977, Pier 9 was the first to have a trunnion installed. Being the smallest, it only weighed 35 tonnes. Sparrows Contract Services set up massive beams spanning the cofferdam, which cantilevered out across the access jetty where the delivery barge was anchored. The trunnion was then raised out of the barge, lowered down into the cofferdam, and placed in its final position in the pier without a hitch. Positioning of the remaining trunnions followed over the next two years, each being carefully manoeuvred into place in the piers within the maximum 3mm tolerance. This was precision engineering at its very best.

Work was also progressing on many other components, including the specialised bearings, generators, electrical switchgear, transformers, control panels and navigation lights in factories all over Britain.

THE ROOFS

The shell roofs had been designed by architects in the GLC Building Department, led by Brian Thaxton, who had considered a wide variety of designs before deciding on the curved housing, clad with stainless steel. The detailed design was given to the Timber Research and Development Association, who asked Bristol University to carry out wind tunnel tests to check the aerodynamics.

The GLC contract for the construction and erection of the roofs was let to Tysons Ltd. of Liverpool. They were experienced fabricators of laminated wood structures, but this would be one of their biggest challenges.

It was a complicated design, with three-dimensional, curved timber frames, nineteen metres high, connected by a triple skin of European redwood boarding to take the hundreds of 600mm-wide stainless steel panels. This meant the panels had to be bent in three dimensions, with no ripples allowed. The panels were joined with standing seams into which clips were folded to secure the sheets to the roof. Each laminated wooden beam had to be bent to shape, using a form to achieve the very exacting tolerances. They had to be trial assembled in Tysons' workshops in Liverpool, then split into smaller sections to be transported to London by barge. It was an enormous challenge for Tysons' craftsmen, and they rose to it spectacularly, creating stunning pieces of craftsmanship.

However, on site in London, the unions were not pleased when they heard the roofs were to be erected by a company from Liverpool. They were of the opinion that local labour should carry out the erection. John Grice decided the way to settle this was to take Adrian Franklin, the union convenor and the works committee to Liverpool to see for themselves. They went to the Tysons workshop and were joined by Pat Healey, the Liverpool UCATT Full Time Official (FTO). When they saw the standard of craftsmanship in the complex geometry of the West African, iroko hardwood, laminated, framed arches, plus the precisely jointed, three-ply redwood planking of the double-curvature decking, they were impressed.

Adrian then asked the union delegation,

'If you had made these, would you let anyone else fit them?'

The answer was a unanimous *'No'*, and Tysons were invited to send their carpenters from Liverpool to complete the erection on site.

The day finished with a tour of Anfield, the famous football ground of Liverpool Football Club, to round off a totally memorable day.

By the end of 1977, Tysons had completed the fabrication of the roof for Pier 9 in Liverpool, apart from some work on the cladding. Once again, due to delays on site, they had to put the roof into storage. It was moved to a large hangar at Speke Airport, (renamed John Lennon Airport in 2001), which attracted many sightseers from Merseyside, who were astonished and delighted at the complexity and quality of the carpenters' handiwork.

AN ALMOST PERFECT STORM

On January 12, 1978, a strong storm surge caused the high-water level at London Bridge to rise to within 300mm of the highest ever recorded. High tide was forecast for midday, and there was panic in the Houses of Parliament as a result. Ministers looked out of their windows and saw the mighty Thames threatening to overflow the embankments. The Ministry of Agriculture and Fisheries hastily convened a meeting to discuss ways of giving top priority to the barrier and get it operable as soon as possible.

I arrived on site before 08:00 that day to a scene of frantic activity. At 10:00 I went down to the access jetty by the Pier 9 cofferdam, and watched the watermen getting the last of the boats to a safe haven, and the foremen evacuating the last of the men out of the cofferdam. You could feel the nervous trepidation throughout the site, but all you could do, (like King Canute,) was watch the water rise as high tide approached, and trust the forecasters had got the timing right.

The Thames estuary turned into a vast, powerful expanse of swiftly moving water, swirling its way towards central London. When the level reached within 500mm of the top of the sheet piles, the murky water streamed through the 30mm-diameter lifting holes of the piles, forming cascading waterfalls around the entire perimeter of the cofferdams. It was a mesmerising sight, and there was absolutely nothing we could do about it. We were watching the full power of Mother Nature flexing her muscles, not even angrily, reminding the civil engineers of our limitations and place. We must respect and enhance the power of Nature, never try to tame it.

Fortunately, the forecasters were right that day, and around midday, when the water level reached 300mm from the top of the piles, the surge tide started to turn and the levels gradually dropped. It was a sobering moment, with sighs of relief all round, and a timely reminder of the importance of our task.

Following this experience, carpenters on the south side spent the remainder of the day in the cofferdams urgently knocking wooden plugs into the lifting holes of the piles. On the north side, the dock sheet piles were also plugged. This increased the tidal protection to the dock by another 500mm, with further protection to the inner berms and the dewatering systems.

Over thirty years later, I was working on the construction of Stonecutter's Bridge in Hong Kong, when a powerful typhoon blew in from the South China Sea. It was the highest signal, Number 12, which occurs around once a decade, when gusts of wind can reach over 200 miles per hour. Mother Nature at her angriest. I was battened down in my apartment on the sixteenth floor, watching in awe as TV satellite dishes were ripped off roof tops below me, and windows were being sucked out of high-rise buildings by powerful gusts of howling wind. The windows of my apartment were taped, but they were still bowing under the pressure.

One of the tallest buildings was the Inland Revenue tower on Hong Kong Island, sixty storeys high. Two floors of windows were sucked out by the powerful vortexes that the typhoon created amongst the tower blocks, and a cascade of paperwork, including thousands of tax returns, fluttered over the city, much to the delight of local taxpayers, and distress of the tax inspectors.

Soon after the surge in January, the government called an urgent meeting in London with the GLC and the PLA, to agree a reduced navigation width at the barrier from 122 metres to 61 metres, This would allow CTHJV to bring forward the date of the second phase of work. General acceptance was quickly reached with the PLA and other shipping interests that a reduced opening could work, but there was concern that there would be a small, but increased risk of collisions. Work starting immediately could possibly knock a year off the barrier programme, and the risk was accepted. It would entail extra cost, and as the two-year agreement with CTHJV was soon to expire, this was an ideal time to start negotiations on how to make this revised programme work.

INCENTIVES

It was accepted by the GLC and the government that the CTHJV would need to wave a reasonable financial carrot to incentivise the whole workforce to finish the job. The solution was to renegotiate the contract, with bonuses to be paid, but only if the barrier was completed on time and within a target cost. This was fixed at £165,000,000 and the barrier would have to be operable by 1982 - 1983. If the cost was either 5% less or 5% more than the target figure, profits or losses would be shared, with a maximum exposure of £12,000,000.

A sliding scale of bonuses was agreed. The GLC and RPT

team put forward a proposal for four successive stages, with time and cost targets with bonuses or penalties, but CTHJV were in a strong negotiating position, and after months of wrangling there was still no agreement.

It went to arbitration and took several months before Patrick Garland, the arbitrator, broke the deadlock and brokered an agreement between the two sides, which was finally concluded in January 1979.

Little information had been leaked to the press, so they had a field day speculating on the amount CTHJV was promising in incentives to complete the project two years early, and there was much criticism of them being too generous. In the end though, this agreement achieved its purpose and the contract finished ahead of schedule.

MOVING FORWARD

South Side

By February 1978, the south abutment, the smallest structure on the south side was complete, and Pier 9 was progressing rapidly. The pier interface section with the sill was complete, and the level where the curved noses of the piers started, had been reached. This allowed metal shutters to be used for the next repetitive lifts, which were quicker to install and gave a finer finish.

The recess for the jacks to install the gate end was formed, and the lift shaft and cable and pipe shafts had started, which meant they would soon reach the machinery rooms. When the structure reached the struts spanning the cofferdam, they were removed, and short stub struts were fitted between the piles of the cofferdam and the external wall of the pier.

Better momentum was being achieved with the three-shift working day, and by the end of March, the main structure of Pier 9 had emerged from the cofferdam. The machinery rooms were completed, and ready to be enshrouded by the timber arch frames, and the shining, stainless-steel clad roof.

Much had been learnt which would benefit the building of subsequent piers, but it would be another nine months before Pier 8 would be complete.

North Side

On the north side, they were also making good progress. More staff were being recruited, including a new pier manager, Rick Randall, who was brought in as part of Warren's team.

Richard Randall, (always known as Rick), was born in Luton, Bedfordshire, in 1945, and went to school in nearby Harpenden. He was an able student and went on to gain an Honours degree in Civil Engineering at Aberdeen University, graduating in 1967.

He started his career with Engineering and Power Development, a design company of Balfour Beatty, working on the civil design of a pump house for the power station for the Alcan aluminium smelter at Lynemouth, in Northumberland. In that office he worked with a senior engineer working for the contractor called Alan Mitchell. Their paths would cross again later when they were recruited by RPT on the barrier.

In 1969 he looked for more site experience, and

joined Balfour Beatty International. For two years he worked on the extension to the Kipevu Power Station in Mombasa, Kenya, on the east coast of Africa. This was his introduction to marine works, working with divers and underwater concrete, and the experience would stand him in good stead for future projects.

On returning from Africa, he joined RPT in London to work on the design of the piers for the Thames Barrier. His boss was Alan Mitchell, who helped him complete the design experience required to become chartered, and gave Rick an excellent training. They were to meet again on the barrier.

In 1973, he rejoined Balfour Beatty to work on a variety of projects around the UK, including as a sub-agent on the second Dartford Tunnel under the River Thames.

Rick was ambitious, and after reading about the Thames Barrier, he contacted the CTHJV to see what positions were available. He was interviewed by John Grice and Warren Hibbs, and was offered a job on the north side as Pier Manager on Pier 3. He accepted immediately.

He arrived on the barrier site just before the dry dock was to be flooded. It was a hive of activity - final checks were being made on the sills, piling was ongoing on the access jetty and the Pier 3 cofferdam, and excavation for the cofferdams for Piers 1 and 2 was under way. Rick was a talented, energetic, popular figure, and by the end of the year, his role was extended to help with the planning for the lowering of the north side sills, and to complete the remaining civil works on the north side.

Rick was closely involved with the lowering of the sills, and from the experience with the lowering of the first sill, recommended moving the start of the programme forward by twelve hours. This meant towing the sills from the King George V dock at night, enabling the lowering of the sill to be carried out in daylight, an exercise that worked much better for the engineering team.

He remained until the completion of the civil works on the north side, and left the barrier in 1981 with a wealth of experience under his belt. He next saw the barrier at its grand opening in 1984.

His next project was as a sub-agent on the construction of the Ipswich by-pass, followed by a series of marine projects. He was Project Manager on the construction of a large, floating dock in Coulport, near Helensburgh, in Scotland, an extension to the repair base for the Trident nuclear submarines. The massive, floating dock had a float-out weight of around 70,000 tonnes, (approximately the weight of the QE2 cruise liner), seven times the weight of the sills on the barrier.

In 1994, the controversial Cardiff Bay Barrage started, and Rick was appointed Construction Manager. The 1.1km-long harbour breakwater was one of the largest projects in the country at the time, and took six years to complete. It met strong opposition from environmental bodies, so a lot of money was spent on creating new habitats for the wildlife. This barrage enabled huge changes in Cardiff and allowed the regeneration of the docks, which have given enormous benefits to the Welsh capital city.

Rick returned to London in 2001 as the contractor's Project Manager for the Channel Tunnel rail link into the terminus at St. Pancras Station, another project with enormous challenges.

In 2006, he was tempted abroad again, to Mexico as the Costain construction manager in a consortium with a large Chinese company, China Harbour, to build the Costa Azul breakwater. This required twelve, massive caissons to be cast in a dry dock, towed out and sunk offshore in the Pacific Ocean. There he was reunited with his old friends, Warren Hibbs and Paul Sivey, the first time they had all worked together since leaving the barrier.

In 2008 Rick set up his own consultancy, and has now retired to the New Forest in Hampshire, to relax at last, play golf, and still be near the sea.

With the agreement of the PLA to reduce the navigation channel in February, this enabled construction of the cofferdam for Pier 3, (identical to Pier 9), to start straight away in the shallow water on the north side of the diversion channel.

The CTHJV design team had completed the modified design using heavier, German, Peine piles, which could be installed quicker by being driven in pairs. They also had two clutches either side of the pile, giving a double skin, which greatly improved the watertightness. The flat face of the piles also made excavation much easier.

Pre-bored holes were drilled into the chalk and bentonite slurry poured in to stiffen the sides of the holes. (Bentonite is a type of volcanic clay that can form a temporary barrier due to its natural ability to absorb large amounts of water). The piles were lifted into place by crane, and driven six metres into the chalk.

The increased thickness of the Peine piles also made them strong enough to only need a single frame of cross struts in Pier 3, saving significant time.

SILL CONSTRUCTION

Before construction started in the dry dock, a 1mm-thick steel plate had been laid down on the casting bed which minimised the breaking force required to lift off and float the sills. This was another time of apprehension for the designers. The force to break this seal between the concrete and the steel membrane was known theoretically, but it was not an exact science, and the force was nearly always greater than estimated. The smaller sills weighed 3,500 tonnes, but the bigger concern was for the largest sills which were 27 metres wide, 8.5 metres high and 61 metres long, weighing around 10,000 tonnes.

The sills had been designed by RPT as cellular structures to reduce their weight to enable them to float, and yet still have enough stiffness. This required longitudinally, post-tensioned cables cast in the full length of the sill, to take the tensile stresses induced both when the sills were floating, and also when they were positioned on the bearings. The cables were supplied and fixed by PSC, a specialist, French sub-contractor who had to fix them to a very tight, vertical profile tolerance, allowing no movement during concreting. After casting, surveyors had to check the external dimensions of the sills meticulously, to double-check the calculated weights of the sills were correct.

By May 1978, the four concrete sills in the dry dock were

complete and final preparations were ongoing to make them watertight and ready for the tow-out. Steel bulkheads were fixed to the scallops of the sill at either end, and hemispherical bulkheads fitted to the access subways.

When this work was complete, the flooding of the dock commenced. A short length of berm and piles was removed on the inside of the dock, wide enough for the sills to be towed out. The water started flowing in, and there was no going back.

As water filled the dock, the designers waited apprehensively to see if they had got their sums right. The smaller sills lifted relatively quickly as the dock filled with water, but as predicted, the larger sills resisted for some time before they detached themselves from the steel sheet and slowly floated to the surface. Despite their initial confidence, the relief from the designers was palpable.

FLOAT OUT TRAGEDY

On June 1, the four sills were ready to be towed out of the flooded dry dock. The operation was under the control of Captain Arthur King, from the sub-contractor Alexander Towing, of Gravesend, using two, powerful sea-going tugs.

Because of the Thames tidal range, and the river currents which affected the tidal forces on the float-outs, it was essential the towing was performed at slack high water, (as the tide is turning). This avoided significant lateral forces on the floating sill, especially when emerging from the dry dock, but there was only a short window of opportunity.

The client decided to make the first tow-out a big event

to celebrate this key date. There was a large gathering of government officials, including representatives from the GLC, local councillors, and the media, assembled on the south side, looking forward to the spectacle. The leader of the GLC, Horace, (later Sir Horace) Cutler, got the ceremony off to a spectacular start by firing off green flares. They went high into the sky from the south bank, over the river and lit up the north bank.

I was more interested in the manoeuvring of the sill out of the dry dock, so I went across to the north side. Massive winches on the tugs started to reel in the thick, heavy, nylon ropes from the sills, by three teams of CTHJV lightermen who were feeding out the ropes from the bollards.

The winches started taking the load of the sill, and you could see the ropes tensioning and taking the strain. The next thing I heard was what sounded like a loud cannon shot, which echoed around the dock. Everything happened very quickly. The rope had snagged around one of the bollards and before it could be cut, it snapped and whiplashed back across the sill.

The lighterman standing nearest to the bollard was Edgar Frederick McGuiness, who took the full force of the whiplash, severing both his legs. He toppled into the water with a sickening splash. Luckily, the two other men standing behind Edgar only received minor injuries.

Within seconds, a rescuer had jumped in with a line, and they were both pulled into the safety boat by the crew. The rescuer was the scaffolding foreman, John Haines, who later received a bravery award for diving to the rescue without regard for his personal safety, with tugs and sills in the immediate vicinity.

The boat took only ten minutes to get across to the south bank, whilst a first-aider desperately tried to apply tourniquets to stop Edgar bleeding to death. Getting the poor man out of the boat and into the ambulance was chaotic, with angry exchanges hurled at the gaggle of press photographers, who surged forward trying to get gory shots for the evening papers. This incensed many of the onlookers. Strong words were exchanged, and shortly afterwards, some expensive cameras were thrown into the dock.

Edgar was given morphine in the ambulance, but sadly, died en-route, despite the hospital being less than ten minutes away.

Edgar was aged fifty-six, and came from Wateringbury, a small, historic village nestling near Maidstone, in Kent. A dark cloud hung over the site, which closed down for the rest of the day in respect. Thanks to the high health and safety standards observed on site, there were no more fatalities on the barrier, an exceptional safety record for those times.

The next day a thorough review of the towage procedures was carried out, concentrating on minimising the use of check lines. This tragedy really affected the morale of the float-out team, but they carried on, and the remaining three sills were towed out without further incident.

The north dock was re-sealed and pumped out by October, ready to start construction of the last two sills.

A CLOSE ENCOUNTER

There was an unexpected and unwelcome surprise to finish the year. It was a cold night on November 11. Thick fog engulfed much of Britain, and swirled across the Thames in dense patches, worthy of a scene from Dicken's *Great Expectations*.

Around midnight, a 7000-tonne Greek cargo ship called *Plotines,* loomed like a ghostly apparition through the murk, towed by two PLA tugs. It had left East India Docks that evening, fully laden with goods destined for Antwerp. The tugs travelled downriver from Bugsby's Reach and turned into Woolwich Reach, but as they headed slowly towards the barrier, they hit a thick patch of fog.

Without warning, the ship veered off course. The tugs' tow ropes snapped, and *Plotines* rammed into a piling barge before crashing into the sheet piles protruding from the south end of the dry dock. This was all observed on the PLA radar, but it happened so quickly, they could do nothing to stop it.

There were over 200 men working inside the floodlit dock that night, including my good friend Sam Cornberg, He recalled the sound of the collision echoing inside the dry dock as terrifying. Thankfully, on that particular night, luck was on their side. There was only one 200-metre section of sheet piles that was double-skinned, and that is what the ship struck. The other sections were single-skinned. The bow of *Plotines* buckled the outer sheet piles but did not penetrate the inner row, avoiding a potential catastrophe.

The bow of the ship was damaged, and it began to list. The tugs quickly threw new lines to *Plotines,* and the ship was swiftly pulled back and towed downriver, disappearing into the black, engulfing fog as quickly as it had appeared. It was towed to Crayfordness to await a marine insurance assessor to arrive from Lloyds of London. Emergency repairs started immediately on the damaged piles of the dry dock, lasting all night, so enabling work on the sills to continue as usual the following day.

The GLC immediately came under fire for pushing the PLA to narrow the navigation channel earlier in the year. The flamboyant leader of the GLC, Sir Horace Cutler, gave a statement to the press admitted the narrowing of the channel could have contributed to the accident, but finished defiantly with,

'...*there is a great threat of a major catastrophe to London if we get a surge tide before the barrier is completed.*'

It had been an exhausting and exhilarating year for all.

8

1979

The year started well, with the agreement between CTHJV and the government signed in January. This allowed for an immediate start of piling for a new shipping fender around Pier 4 to narrow down the navigation channel to 61 metres, in preparation for the switch of navigation channels later that summer.

With a minimum of fourteen million pounds extra promised by the government to achieve the key dates, the next vital step was for CTHJV to get a mutually rewarding settlement with the 1400 operatives on site. A programme was drawn up for negotiation with the unions, setting out seven key objectives to the contract completion, with an agreed reduction in the numbers of workers at each stage.

AGREEMENT

In March, John Grice led a team of senior managers to work through all the details with the five unions, led by their negotiator, Bruce Birdsell. On May 18, 1979, after two months of tough bargaining, a Site Supplemental Agreement was signed. The seven key stages to completion were agreed, with each stage having a bonus of £500 paid to every employee on site, from the teaboy to the section manager, and an incremental number of workers being made redundant.

A green book was produced entitled, 'General Conditions of Employment and the Site Supplemental Agreement' and issued to everyone on site. John Grice requested particular cooperation on twenty-three items set out in the green book, with two he considered vital. First, that the fifteen-minute shift handover at the place of work be implemented diligently and second, that the restrictive practices and covert industrial action should cease immediately.

Meal breaks had been another contentious issue on the twelve-hour shift, with significant time lost due to the number of rest periods required, and the time getting to the canteens and back. On the new system, there was one tea and one meal break period per eight-hour shift, and canteens were moved closer to the work areas where possible.

The first key date was to be four months later, on July 16, 1979, for the switching of the navigation channels.

The agreement transformed the project, with an incentive for the entire work force to hit the key dates, where everyone would benefit. The union squabbling stopped overnight, and progress improved noticeably over the next few months.

PORT OF LONDON AUTHORITY (PLA)

The PLA kept a close watch on all the works being carried out on the river around the barrier, and regular liaison meetings were held with RPT and CTHJV. I was told of one unusual meeting that was called a few months before the switch of the navigation channels. Adrian Franklin and Paul Sivey represented CTHJV and travelled to a PLA office which was in an office block in outer London, with the meeting being held on an upper floor overlooking the Thames.

They were gathered round a large table with plans of the river laid out before them, with Adrian and Paul sitting facing the window. The detailed discussions had been going on for some time, when Paul suddenly glanced up and to his astonishment saw a body hurtle past the window at great speed. He looked at Adrian, and by the look of disbelief on his face, he realised Adrian had seen it too. On looking closer out of the window they could only see a small chimney, but no sign of a body. The meeting came to an end, and they returned to site none the wiser.

The following morning was the first Saturday in the month. Aerial photographs needed to be shot for the monthly report and Adrian had been invited to go up in the helicopter with the pilot. They met at a nearby helipad, and Adrian found, to his consternation, that he had a seat adjacent to the photographer, which required the doors to be open, meaning his legs were dangling out into space. It was an exhilarating ride, and gave amazing views into the city, and out east towards Tilbury Docks. On landing, Adrian asked the helicopter pilot if he had ever had any unusual requests. His reply stunned him. The pilot mentioned that only the day before, he had been asked to help on the new James Bond film in outer London, and had to drop a body down a chimney, very close to an office block!

A SPECIAL VISITOR

1979 saw a major upheaval in UK politics, resulting in some unexpected visitors coming to the site over the next few months.

It had been a hard, cold winter, and in January, Jim Callaghan, the Labour Prime Minister, was struggling with the 'Winter of Discontent.' There were crippling strikes in many quarters, including the railways, water, haulage, nurses, ambulances, refuse collectors and grave diggers. Inflation had fallen to under 10%, but pay rises were kept to a minimum, leaving many struggling. In 1974, at the age of fifty, Margaret Thatcher had become leader of the Conservative Party after overthrowing Edward Heath, and was ambitious for power.

On March 28 1979, she harnessed enough support in Parliament to win a vote of no confidence in the failing Labour government. A general election was called for on May 3, with the previous month occupied by hard canvassing.

At the beginning of the year, the 'Iron Lady' realised it would be to her political advantage to show a more compassionate side to her abrasive style. She needed a new, softer image, and the advertising company Saatchi and Saatchi was brought in to assist. The transformation included a complete makeover - her wardrobe, her hair, and above all, her voice. She now needed some low profile visits to try out this new persona.

On February 22, security tightened noticeably on the site, with more searches and identity checks made, so we knew someone of importance was about to visit. It was a gloomy spring morning, and a small cavalcade of cars swept through the south side entrance and parked near the access jetty. A welcome committee lined up to greet the person who many knew very little about, and cared even less. Margaret Thatcher bounded out of her car enthusiastically, closely followed by her nervous entourage. She was wearing a blue suit and gold brooch, and her new, softer hairstyle was clearly sprayed into position to counter any river breezes.

She walked swiftly to the line of representatives from the GLC and RPT, and a few CTHJV senior managers waiting to greet her. Thatcher was already notorious for not sticking to the carefully orchestrated line-ups, and looked for people who interested her.

After brief introductions to the managers, she turned and headed straight for a group of startled workers, who were definitely not on the agenda, and with her perfected, coiffed look, enquired what they were doing, and told them how important they were to the country. The last man she reached, Tom Ennis, had a great girth and loomed over her. He dipped as if to bow, but it looked more like a curtsy, and said confidently,

'It's a pleasure to meet the next Prime Minister.'

She was delighted, and rushed on without witnessing him being harangued by his irate fellow workers.

Thatcher spotted an access ladder to one of the pier super-structures and scurried over to it, followed by a snaking line of rapidly panicking aides. She was half a dozen steps up before the first horror-stricken assistant caught up, and desperately clasped hold of her legs to prevent any opportunist photographer causing an embarrassment. This amused her, and she continued climbing, with the desperate aide begging her to come down.

She returned to earth, and was escorted to the RPT office where she met the Resident Engineer, George Davies and his senior managers to hear them explain the workings of the barrier. She absorbed the information quickly and came back with intelligent questions - a refreshing change from the average politician.

A few months later she won the election, and became Prime Minister with an agenda that would rip the nation apart for generations.

I met Lady Thatcher, (as she had become) in Hong Kong in 1997, when she was invited to open two impressive bridges, part of the Lantau Link leading to the new airport that was still under construction. I was working on the massive double-decker Kap Shui Mun Bridge, with six lanes of motorway on top, and two railway tracks running through it.

The Tsing Ma suspension bridge, 97 metres longer than the Golden Gate Bridge in San Francisco, adjoined it, and was being built by a Costain-Mitsui JV, with Alistair Handford the project manager. Most of the deck steelwork was fabricated and erected by Cleveland Bridge at the same yard as the barrier gates, in Darlington.

Dick Thorp, was the project manager for Cleveland Bridge, who had been the site manager for the erection of the gates on the barrier. The Chinese were so impressed with the Tsing Ma Bridge that they copied it in Southern China, even using some of the Cleveland workers for the spinning of the cables.

In 1992, Lady Thatcher made a visit to Paris, which gave the many disgruntled members of the Tory cabinet the opportunity to make their move, and got a vote of no confidence in her passed in Parliament. One of the leaders of the coup was Chris Patten, who subsequently lost his seat in the next election a few months later, and accepted the post of the last Governor of Hong Kong.

As Lady Thatcher had been a key figure in the negotiations leading to the Sino-British Joint Declaration in 1984, she followed events in Hong Kong very closely, and visited the colony several times. By 1997, Lady Thatcher had come to terms with her demise, and had almost forgiven Chris Patten for his leading part in the treachery, but she still enjoyed the spotlight.

Later that year, she arrived in Hong Kong on April 26 to participate in the opening of the two new bridges, and the Governor gave a lavish dinner in her honour, with 160 guests attending. The following day she was taken to the viewing point overlooking the two bridges in a small bus with Chris Patten. She alighted, more slowly this time, to meet a line of dignitaries waiting for her. The mischievous glint was in her eye again, and she shot off in the opposite direction to talk to a small group of startled engineers from the British designers, Mott MacDonald, One was Bill Reynolds, who had worked on the barrier with RPT. Once again, she had done her homework, and quizzed them with unexpected questions, showing she still hadn't lost her touch.

That evening, Lady Thatcher pressed a button with Chris Patten and Anson Chan, (the Head of the Hong Kong Civil Service) to open the two bridges. This lit up the 206m-high towers and the suspension cables of Tsing Ma in a breathtaking array of pulsating colours, and this was followed by a cavalcade of luxury cars and an open-topped Rolls Royce engulfed in streamers and confetti. The finale was a spectacular fireworks display from three barges, lined up behind the bridges, which included a cascading waterfall from the Tsing Ma deck, accompanied by a compilation of stirring classical music pieces.

I was on a boat in the harbour on that spectacular night, and it reminded me of the special day the barrier was officially opened, but not as cold.

PROGRESS

On the north side, the main structures of Piers 1 and 2 were started in January and completed by the end of the year.

On the south side, the main structure for Pier 6 and Pier 8 was complete by the end of January. In April, work on the main structure of Pier 7 was also finished.

Everyone now concentrated on completing the switch of the navigation channel, to hit Key Date 1 by July.

The critical structure to complete was Pier 5. To get access to this pier, the northern navigation channel had to be switched to the south between Pier 6 and Pier 7. This required the removal of the cofferdams around these piers.

There were very few companies in this country willing to do it. Enter Reg Clucas and his specialised team of divers from Hull in East Yorkshire, who were famous for taking on high risk jobs that few others would touch.

They had to cut through the bottom of the sheet piles, one metre below river bed level, with white-hot thermic lances, which was difficult, extremely hot, and high risk. Nobody envied their job, but when they succeeded, it enabled the first key date to be achieved on June 16, 1979, two weeks early, much to everybody's delight. Consequently, enthusiastic celebrations went on in the Barrier Arms late into the night.

The paying of the bonus payments to the workforce presented its own special problems. At that time, fewer people had bank accounts, so wages were all paid weekly in cash in a wage packet. The workforce was 2000 strong and everyone received the first bonus payment of £500. This meant that, on that day, around one million pounds was being brought to the site by road. Naturally, there was great concern about security as the movement of this amount of cash would no doubt have attracted the attention of the criminal gangs in London, especially the Krays and the Richardsons, who still had influence even though the leaders were all serving long stretches in prison. The security van carrying the cash was given an armed escort through east London from the bank to the site, and armed guards were stationed on site all day whilst the workers were being paid. There was also concern for the men after they had been paid, as they would have been easy targets on leaving the site.

The security van arrived on site without incident and, as far as I know, the workers all got home safely that night.

SILL LOWERING

All eyes were now on the sill team for the lowering of the first sill into position.

Detailed planning had gone into this operation led by Aarvid Degonaars and his Dutch team with their vast marine knowledge, supported by Warren Hibbs, leading the managers and engineers from the other CTHJV partners.

The first sill to be lowered into its final resting place was between Pier 8 and Pier 9, in span B. It was one of the smaller sills, 31.5 metres long, but it still weighed around 3,500 tonnes.

A control centre had been set up in portacabins adjacent to Pier 9 to oversee the operation. Many of the engineers and technicians knew that the next twenty-four hours would be some of the most stressful of their lives.

The sill for span B had been moored up in King George V dock for over a year, and on September 5, it was carefully eased through the lock gates and into the Thames by tugs ensuring it was kept well clear of the dock walls. This operation would be far trickier with the larger sills, as they would have only just over a metre of clearance to spare.

The procession set off slowly upriver, the sill being towed by five tugs. Two large tugs were twenty metres in front, attached by thick ropes to the front bollards, pulling the sill. Two smaller ones were positioned against the sides to help control sideways movement. A fifth was centrally placed twenty metres behind the sill, attached by ropes to prevent the back from drifting.

Within two hours the tugs arrived at the waiting area down-river from the barrier, where they anchored, in preparation for the rising tide, when the sill could be winched over the stubs of the cut cofferdam walls on the river bed into its lowering position.

The winches were provided and operated by Sparrows, the specialist lifting and rigging contractor based in Bath, Somerset, providing equipment handling services, especially for the oil and gas industries. Their operator was in the control cabin alongside the rest of the CTHJV team.

When the sill was in position, the lowering of the sills was carried out by a French sub-contractor, PSC, who provided the specialist cables and jacking equipment, with their personnel also stationed in the control cabin.

The sill was positioned over a dredged trench, where a stone-bed layer had been placed on the bottom of the trench. The level of the stone had been carefully controlled using a steel beam suspended beneath a boat, and checked by divers to ensure there were no high spots. Sand would be pumped in under high pressure at a later date.

It was essential the lowering jacks were connected during the falling tide so that no load was taken. When low tide was reached water was pumped into the scallop. This allowed the sill to lose its buoyancy, and it became suspended in the water on the cables.

Timing was all. If the descent was too slow, the cables would take the entire weight of the 3,500-tonne sill and become overloaded, and that would have been disastrous. It was a tense time for the team.

For a short time on the decent, the vertical cables started vibrating, which caused concern, but this was soon corrected and the remainder of the operation went well, with the sill landing perfectly on the bearing jacks.

These special jacks had been positioned on the plinths under each corner of the sill. They were in pairs and circular, one metre in diameter, and made up of two thin discs of steel, sealed around the edges. At the beginning of the next rising tide, the sill was slowly lowered into its final resting position.

A final check for position was made with grid lines drawn on the access subways in the piers, lining up with similar grid lines marked on the subway bulkheads in the sill.

A liquid resin was pumped at high pressure into the small space between the discs, which fixed the precise position of the sill.

The painstaking operation took nearly twenty-four hours, and the team was exhausted, but the whole operation was a resounding success. It was a tribute to the technical brilliance of the combined team of Dutch and British engineers that had taken a year of meticulous planning to fit the sill so perfectly in position.

Once the alignment was finalised, the bulkheads were removed and flexible rubber bellows inside each pier subway could be released and connected to the sill subway.

A few weeks later, after the temporary works had been removed around the piers, a specialist Dutch team carried out a high-pressure sand pumping procedure into the stone bed under the sill. A sand-flow barge was moored at a convenient point nearest to the span, and flexible pipes were strung across to the pier, and down into the sill.

The design of the sills had allowed pumping points at regular places along the bottom of the cells, with built-in pipe connections. The sand was piped in under high pressure, filling any voids in the bedding stone until it reached apertures cast in the walls of the cell. This method had been perfected in Holland, with submerged tube tunnels, and the team was under the supervision of Chris Gane, one of the senior CTHJV marine engineers.

After any remaining temporary works were removed, including the access jetties, the bed protection consisting of reed and willow mattresses covered in rock were installed upriver and downriver of the sill by HAM-ACZ dredging, to ensure there would be no scour.

One month later the second sill was lowered into position in span C between Piers 7 and 8. This was the first of the longer sills, 61 m long, using the same team, and with the knowledge gained on the first sill, its precise positioning was another triumph.

SOCIAL EVENTS

With such continuous, intensive pressures exerted on the work force throughout the project, it was essential to have somewhere to relax for a few hours, to mull over the problems thrown up during the day, or to celebrate a success. This was usually in one of the preferred local pubs within walking distance of the site.

The nearest at that time was *The Victoria*, on the corner of Eastmoor Street was a small, late-Victorian pub, built around 1881, with a battered, Edwardian, tiled façade and a tired-looking Truman eagle perched above the pub sign. From my memory, the interior was a large room with a bar to the right. The amenable landlord was ready to adapt to any occasion, at any time, and the pub often remained open into the early hours. It had a few riverside mementoes displayed on the walls, including a set of long oars donated by the watermen after a win in one of the barge races. It could only accommodate a maximum of 100 people, so was often full. Since those heady days, it has suffered two serious fires, and is now, sadly, a burnt-out shell, but the external structure is salvageable. In 2022 there were new plans to resurrect it, keeping the original façade and hopefully, install some reminders of its historic past.

The second was The Horse and Groom, (generally known as The House of Gloom), a larger, more traditional Victorian pub with a long, curved bar and nicotine-stained ceilings and walls. They served ales and lager of variable quality in a smoky, noisy atmosphere, and sold curling, day-old sandwiches, three flavours of crisps, one type of nuts, and some ancient pickled onions fermenting in a jar on the bar. In the corner was an old juke box playing the hits of 1979 - *YMCA* by Village People, *Tragedy* by the Bee Gees, *I Will Survive* by Gloria Gaynor, *Do Ya Think I'm Sexy* by Rod Stewart, newcomers Dire Straits with *Sultans of Swing* and Blondie's *Heart of Glass*.

On one of the walls was a darts board, popular with the locals. One of the carpenters' foremen, recently returned from building a large dam in Sri Lanka, decided to introduce his overseas version of darts to the locals. He played with six-inch nails. On his first pint he was deadly accurate, and much admired for his javelin skills. By the time he was on the third pint, his aim was not so good and hard hats were required, as the steel missiles ricocheted off the board around the bar, impaling anyone standing too near. The landlord banned him when a dart destroyed an optic one night, sending a litre of five-star whisky cascading onto the floor.

A little further along the river was The Hope and Anchor, another interesting, historical, riverside pub which went back to Tudor times, but was rebuilt in 1899. It underwent further changes after World War II when a V1 flying bomb, (known as a doodlebug) hit the glassworks behind the pub, causing substantial damage, necessitating another rebuild.

They served traditional English fare, and the pub was popular in the summer as you could sit outside, enjoy a good view downriver and the watch the piers rising majestically out of the river. The downside was that you did have to prepare yourself to be engulfed by occasional sickly wafts of sweet, malty vapour from processing sugar beet, drifting across from the Tate and Lyle factory on the other side of the river. I was pleased to read The Hope and Anchor is still flourishing today, but now customers are overlooked by luxury blocks of flats, and the views are of a new environmental park adjacent to the barrier.

1979 WOBBLER AWARDS

Since 1977, a much-anticipated ceremony called The Wobbler Awards was held just before Christmas. It was to celebrate the less successful innovations and management initiatives of that year.

It had a certain Pythonesque quality about it, possibly as it was set up by a small committee from the wet section, led by Senior Wobbler, Gavin Maxwell-Hart, a multi-winning recipient for his various innovations. When the wet section was going through the cofferdam excavation difficulties in the early days, some extraordinary, Heath Robinson excavating tools were welded together and tried out, with enthusiastic optimism, and eventual disappointment. Other departments were now strong contenders for prizes, so the venue was the large, welders' shop to accommodate a greater number of people.

The presentations were made by Fred Day, a natural stand-up entertainer from the Commercial Department, relishing his role as MC in a one-hour special.

In 1979, the coveted first prize went to senior Commercial Manager, David Jenkins, for special services to the PLA for his overwhelming generosity in the hiring of some of the biggest and most expensive cranes in Europe. He received a Lego, Samson crane to remind him of his magnificent contribution.

The second prize went to Ray Genoni, whose attempts to transfer the offices and staff from the south side to the north created total chaos without any effort whatsoever. He remained completely unfazed and considered it a great honour to be nominated for the award. We could only put this down to his Italian ancestry.

Third prize was won by the suave and unflappable Construction Manager, Warren Hibbs, for his ability to control the team of sill-sinking smurfs, who were continually solving mind-boggling puzzles, mostly of their own making.

Special awards also went to Construction Manager, Adrian Franklin, for his uncannily real impersonation of John Grice, and Design Manager, Don Langdown, for wearing a pristine, Savile Row suit while inspecting cofferdams. (He was awarded a pair of pinstripe wellies.) Chris Gane won for absent-mindedly marooning a crane on an access jetty which was being dismantled, and had no way of retrieving it.

Rick Randall won an award for best newcomer. The following year, he was disqualified for having the audacity to try to win an award for the underwater self-stacking barges' system, after his team managed to sink two barges at the same time, where one landed on top of the other!

The final award went to the Press Officer, Peter Blaseby, for inaccurately reporting the majority of the 1978 Wobbler Awards, and having no remorse.

It was a full-house, and the whole entertaining evening was a well-earned release from the tensions of a very productive year.

9

1980 – 81

1980

The year opened with the spotlight shifting from the CTHJV civil works to the arrival of the first of the roofs from Tysons, followed by the DCBC gates. The Pier 9 roofs had been in storage since 1977, and it was a relief to Tysons when they were finally eased out of the hangar at Speke Airport in January 1980, and brought down from Liverpool by road, and delivered to site in February. To ensure there would be no problems on the journey, an identical lorry was used, loaded with a framework which replicated the width and height of the roofs, and driven the entire route to London to double check clearances under bridges and positions of road furniture. There was particular concern that where motorway resurfacing had been carried out, which may have diminished the advertised clearances.

CTHJV had completed the machinery rooms. They were ready to be enclosed in their timber shells and made watertight.

All the main players were now on site, and all had interlinking critical dates to meet. It was another tense and busy time.

CIVIL WORKS

CTHJV were working hard to hit all the deadlines for Key Date 2 in April 1980.

This required the south access jetty to be removed and the Pier 5 cofferdam piling to be completed. On the north side, the north abutment, Piers 1 and 2 structures had to be completed, and on the south side, Piers 6 to 9 superstructures had to be finished. It involved every CTHJV section working to their limit, but everything was completed on March 3. It vindicated the use of the bonus as a powerful incentive to drive them on.

As each pier was completed, Reg Clucas moved in to cut the piles of the cofferdams. The PLA required the piles be cut off one metre below river bed level, to avoid any risk of scour uncovering the pile stump. This meant the piles had to be cut from inside the cofferdams. The first cofferdams used the lighter, Larsen piles, which the divers cut horizontally with thermic oxygen lances. Space was constricted and conditions were difficult, but nothing compared to cutting the much heavier, double-skinned, Peine piles. This again required the services of Reg Clucas and his specialist diving team.

A bold, (some thought crazy) solution was put forward by Reg. An initial access hole could be made on the inside face of the pile in the cofferdam for the diver to squeeze inside the box with the thermic lance, and cut the external wall. It would be very restricted, hot, claustrophobic, and high risk. It would need a cool head. The cut needed to be stepped, made through adjacent piles, one pair being cut at the lowest level and the next pair at the highest, right round the perimeter.

As the clutches of the piles were still interlocked, the piles were still stable at that point. The cofferdam could then be flooded, the horizontal stub struts removed by the divers, and the sections of the piles above the cut level removed by crane. The supervising managers were a lot more nervous than Reg, as he cut his way into the boxes. It resembled a scene from Danté's *Inferno*. It was difficult to watch, but Reg had assessed the risk, and it worked.

Once the cofferdam was removed, the installation of the stainless-steel roofs could start. The permanent cranes had been installed on the top roof slabs of Pier 7, Piers 8 and 9 during the first few months, and tracks laid into the machinery rooms. Once again, very fine tolerances were required, ready for the installation of the gate driving rams and crossheads.

Barges carrying the sections of the roof were moored next to the pier and each section lifted off by crane. As each shell roof was completed, this allowed the specialist machinery contractors to start delivering and installing the mechanical and electrical works. This enabled DCBC to start their work.

GATE INSTALLATIONS

Cleveland Bridge had been waiting patiently in Darlington while all the civil works problems were being resolved. The ten gates and twelve, massive disc-shaped mounting arms had been completed for some time, and were mounting up huge storage and re-handling costs, already totalling some £4.9m.

The Cleveland Bridge erection team finally arrived on site in May 1980 to prepare to install gates and machinery in the three southern spans A, B and C. The smaller, falling radial gate was for span A, and the rising sector gates were for spans B and C.

Cleveland had brought their own erection teams, and the managers had to check carefully that the pay rates were compatible with the rest of the barrier force. Luckily, all the Cleveland workers were members of an affiliated union to CTHJV, so that eliminated any disputes.

In June, the gates and mounting arms for spans A, B and C were loaded onto a specially chartered 6000-tonne barge at Port Clarence, using six, multi-wheeled bogies with over 600 wheels, for the final journey to the barrier.

Many of the Cleveland Bridge workers had been closely involved with the gates for years, on one of the most demanding jobs of their lives. They were sad to see them go. This was summed up by the project supervisor, John Robbins and the project engineer, Richard Hand who said at the time,

'When you've lived with a project on and off for so many years, you develop a strange attachment to it. Every one of us that worked on it sweated blood to get it right. I can't deny that seeing the last gate float away was a sad moment in many ways.'

A great deal of careful pre-planning had gone into the fixing of the gate mounting arms, which was a far more complicated operation than the installation of the gates themselves. The fitting of the 31.5-metre falling radial gate in span A, and the first rising sector gate in span B went smoothly. The mounting arm in span B was a mere 300 tonnes.

A greater challenge came with the fitting of the much bigger gate arms on span C between Piers 7 and 8. They were 24.4m-diameter discs, 1.5 metres thick, and loaded with 500 tonnes of cast iron balance weights. Each arm weighed a total of 1100 tonnes.

This needed two, giant, Hebes floating cranes from Hamburg to complete the operation, which required 300 tonnes of specially developed lifting gear. They were some of the biggest in Europe, and worked in tandem to lift the arms, (weighing the equivalent of about 100 London Routemaster buses).

They lifted the first massive disc from the barge, and manoeuvred it over to Pier 8. It was offered up against the concrete, and set down tight against the recess with just 50mm clearance. From here it was slowly lowered onto two jack packs which could make the final adjustments. This gate arm fitted perfectly for Pier 8, but on Pier 7 there was a problem.

As the disc was being lowered, it momentarily touched down on just one side of the jack packs, throwing all 1400tonnes onto the one pack. The jack pack was crushed immediately, and both the very expensive Hebes cranes had to sit for days holding the disc whilst the jack pack was replaced. As there was a likelihood that this could delay the installation of the gate for span C, the GLC insisted the operation be abandoned. It was imperative there should be no delay to the river traffic switch from span D, which was due to take place a few months later. This would enable CTHJV to go ahead with the more critical operation of sinking the sill on span D in early 1981. The gate for span C was taken back to the King George V dock to be stored until it could be installed the following year. It proved to be the right decision.

It wasn't entirely bad news for Cleveland Bridge. A year later, there was a dock strike on Teesside, which was nothing to do with Cleveland, but it meant delivery of the last four gates from Port Clarence was delayed by sixteen weeks. However, having the span C gate at the barrier meant the workforce could keep going, and not be stood down. From the experience of the first gate arm, Cleveland also realised they needed their own diver to assist in fitting the gate arm, and had a man trained up by the Don Shiers team, who were still busy on site.

COMPLETION OF THE PIERS

The Pier 5 team benefitted from the experience of the previous piers, and made rapid progress. The new Peine piles used for the cofferdam speeded up the completion of the piling. There was no buckling of the piles, minimal leakage problems, and the excavation was much easier. As a result, the underwater concrete was poured in June, and broke all pouring records, reaching $90m^3$ an hour. I worked on that final underwater pour, and it was extremely satisfying watching everything working so smoothly.

Dewatering went without a hitch, and construction of Pier 5 was able to start in July. The experienced team hit the ground running, led by the pier manager, Alistair Handford, who had been through all the problems on Pier 9. In one outstanding week in late summer, a whole month's work was completed, breaking all records. It had become a very slick operation.

Key Date 3 was all about the north side. It required both the construction of sills and the Pier 3 superstructure to be completed, the north dock to be removed and Pier 4 underwater concrete finished, all by July.

They all completed early, with the last operation on June 30.

In August, the last two sills were floated out of the dry dock, and the dismantling of the dock began. It had been home for many, for five long and arduous years.

MECHANICAL AND ELECTRICAL

The GLC was concerned that there was only a year in which to get all the mechanical assembly completed, as well as installing the high-pressure hydraulics on the piers. There was limited room on top of the piers and everything had to be craned off a barge and manhandled into the machine rooms. None of the work could be started until all the CTHJV work was finished and the timber roofs were installed. A combination of specialist sub-contractors could then move in to install the machinery, hydraulic cylinders, crossheads, links and much more. These included:

Balfour Kilpatrick: Mechanical and Electrical services
GEC Distribution Switchgear: High voltage switchgear and transformers
Sunderland Forge: Low voltage switchgear
British Brown Boveri: Local control panels
Henry Williams: Control Panels and Equipment
Mirrlees Blackstone: Diesel generators

Thousands of items of equipment had to be delivered to the correct pier, and vitally, in the right order. It was another great achievement by CTHJV and RPT that management of the logistics ensured seamless collaboration between all the contractors involved.

FAREWELLS

There were well-deserved celebrations as each of the Key Dates was achieved, and the bonus money was much welcomed, especially by the younger engineers. For many this windfall meant they could afford to step onto the housing ladder during the huge inflation rises of the 1970s.

It also meant it was the start of the lay-offs, and many staff and workers left CTHJV by the end of 1980. That included me, after the successful final underwater concrete pour on Pier 5.

The barrier created another unexpected bonus for me. It was where I met my wife, Jane, who was one of the office secretaries. She was a very attractive woman, with a style that attracted many admirers, some unwelcome, which she rebuffed with firmness and humour. Jane had never worked on a building site before, but the location was convenient for her at that time, and I was amazed at her adaptability. She would attend the various social events, and it was at one of these, in a smoky bar in Charlton, that we clicked. She had a wonderful sense of humour, hated pompousness, and was an expert in winding up those that deserved it.

It was extremely difficult keeping our relationship quiet on site. You think you are being discreet, but half the office knew very quickly, especially those in the typing pool, who were delighted with the romance and intrigue. We went to the 1979 Christmas dinner and dance together held at the Connaught Rooms in London, where hundreds attended. Jane looked stunning, and I felt a very proud man. We were married shortly afterwards, and enjoyed eighteen wonderful years together.

With so many people working on the barrier over five years, it was inevitable that there were going to be numerous relationships. Several marriages were celebrated. Sam Cornberg married Bridget at an excellent wedding in Blackheath, with many friends coming from the barrier to a memorable, raucous reception near the heath. Alistair Handford married Ann, and shortly afterwards, Paul Sivey married Maggie, sporting an impressive black eye from his previous weekend's rugby activities. I believe Carol Wilson also married that year, to another engineer, Brian Butcher.

One memorable occasion, fellow engineer, Bob Trotter, invited Jane and I to his wedding. I had worked with Bob on Pier 9. He hailed from the Yorkshire Dales and was marrying his childhood sweetheart, who came from the next valley, and they had both been working in London.

The wedding was between Christmas and the New Year in his village. It had been pouring it down for days, and it was a long and challenging car journey from London. We drove up the motorway through torrential rain that turned to sleet and snow the further north we went. We had booked into a large pub in the village, which had been recommended to us, and we arrived in the evening after a fraught journey, both cold and hungry.

On entering the pub, we were greeted warmly by the landlord, who presented us with a delicious, hot plate of pie and Yorkshire caviar (mushy peas), accompanied by a fine pint of Theakstons ale, and a roaring log fire. We only knew a few of the wedding guests, and soon realised we were the only southerners in the pub, the majority coming from Yorkshire and Scotland. It just so happened there was another event taking place that evening, with preparations for the Yorkshire arm-wrestling championships getting underway, sponsored by Theakstons, and the competition was open to both men and women!

The majority of the pub was expected to join in, and couples were randomly paired off. I was drawn against the large, muscle-bound Yorkshire arm-wrestling champion for the first round, who was rather apologetic as he almost broke my arm in under five seconds. My only consolation was that he went on to win.

Jane was paired off with a local girl. I expected her to join me at the bar shortly afterwards but to my surprise, there was no sign of her. Half an hour passed, and I suddenly heard a thunderous cheer. Jane was in the final against the women's champion, a stout, muscular Yorkshire woman, who was also the wife of the men's champion. I was astonished! The crowd were cheering Jane on, in true British fashion, and even more astounded when she held the champion to a draw on her right arm, despite her slim physique. Jane lost on the left arm, but by the cheers of the crowd, you would have thought she had won, much to the chagrin of the winner. I was incredulous and left the pub in even greater awe of my wife than when I arrived.

Most of those leaving that year had been working on the job for nearly five years, and had experienced many ups and downs. We left with many striking memories and lifelong friends. It was a unique experience and an honour to be part of a remarkable project that I would never forget.

1981

This year was critical to the deadline of getting the barrier operating in 1982. Everyone rose to the challenge, with the 61-metre sill for span D, between Piers 6 and 7, lowered into position on March 20. This enabled the navigation channel to be switched to span D.

COMPLETION OF THE PIERS AND SILLS

With the operations working like clockwork, it just got better. The sills for span G were lowered into place in June, span E in July and span F completed on October 1. This last sill was completed with half the staff, and in half the time of the first sill, span B.

Pier progress was also going well, with Pier 4 superstructure completed in April. The last concrete pour, on Pier 5, was celebrated on June 8, months ahead of the Key Date 4 target. By December, span H (between Piers 2 and 3) was also complete on the north side, achieving Key Date 5.

All the bellow connections between the piers and sills were completed, and opened up access for the cable trays to be fixed inside the subway tunnels, for the hundreds of miles of cabling to be installed.

INSTALLATION OF THE GATES

By the end of October, DCBC could at last start the installation of the gates.

The gate ends for Piers 6 and 7 arrived from Port Clarence, and were placed in position in early November. The gate was supposed to follow, but it was delayed due to a dock dispute on Teesside. A swift decision was made that the first gate to be fitted would be between Piers 7 and 8 (span C), which had been moored up in the King George V dock for nearly a year.

In early December, the barge with the 61m-long gate was towed very slowly out of the King George V dock and positioned in front of span C. The plan was to lift it in on December

14, but Mother Nature was not going to make it that easy.

It was the coldest December since 1890, with record-breaking frosts, and ice-cold, northerly winds from Greenland bringing continuous snow cover across much of Britain. The cold spell started on December 6, and heavy snow fell across all of southern England five days later. In many places temperatures fell to between minus ten and minus twenty degrees centigrade at night, making working conditions extremely challenging. Bitter, easterly winds (the Beast from the East) blew on the night of December 13 bringing another coating of snow, but the weather forecast predicted a temporary respite the following morning. As a result, the bold decision was taken to go ahead with the lifting.

By seven o'clock the next morning, the biting Arctic wind had dropped. The two, giant floating, Hebes cranes lifted the 1400-tonne gate, shrouded in a deep layer of snow, off the barge in tandem, ready to move it into position. An hour later, the weak winter's sun shone, the snow melted, and the final decision was taken to complete the operation. The Hebes barges moved their precious load slowly between the piers, and lowered it gently into place onto the two gate ends. By midday, the first gate was secured in place, only hours before the bad weather closed in again.

John Fletcher, Chairman of the DCBC consortium, Bill Maisey the Project Director, and Dick Thorp, the site manager with his excellent team, breathed a sigh of relief, ready to relax and enjoy their Christmas. It was a fine finish to a hectic year, and set everything up for the final push in 1982.

SECURITY

Understandably, there was always a strong security presence on the barrier site, and for just reason. Due to what became known as Bloody Sunday, the Provisional IRA (Irish Republican Army) stepped up bombing attacks in England, especially in London, and particularly on those places with military connections.

On January 30, 1972 there was a demonstration in Belfast by 10,000 Roman Catholic civil rights supporters, which started peacefully, but turned violent, with a hail of stones and Molotov cocktails being thrown at the British soldiers. Some of the British paratroopers opened fire, and thirteen protesters were killed. There was outrage in Northern Ireland, and around the world, which precipitated further support for the IRA, who advocated stepping up the violence in England. Its reign of terror was to continue for the next twenty years.

From 1972, there were many attacks in London, starting with a car bomb planted outside the Old Bailey, injuring 180 people, and another in Whitehall, which wounded another thirty. In August and September of 1973, another forty bombs exploded all over London with many people injured. The attacks extended to railway stations, Heathrow Airport, large department stores such as Harrods and Selfridges, the Bank of England, and the Duke of York's barracks in Chelsea, causing fear, misery, resentment and death.

The year ended with a huge car bomb being placed at the Royal Artillery barracks at Woolwich in December, only a few miles from the barrier site, when five people were injured in the blast. In November 1974, a stick of gelignite was thrown through the window of the King's Arms pub in Woolwich.

Two people were killed, a gunner in the Royal Artillery, and a 20-year-old sales clerk. Thirty-five others were injured, including the landlady.

In 1973, I was working with a consultant in London, and my office overlooked Victoria train station. The station was often targeted. There were many false alarms, and we all became rather blasé. Every morning, we would place bets on how many times the station would be closed. It was five one day, and many times we saw the Army looking for explosives, with messages frequently broadcast over the tannoy system to look out for unattended briefcases or luggage. On several occasions there were controlled explosions, with sandwiches and paper scattering like confetti over the platforms. It always amazed me how quickly people adapted to these conditions and carried on working, determined not to be intimidated.

My closest encounter to the bombing campaign was in 1977, when I was working on the barrier, and I was living in a bedsit in Blackheath with a good view over London. It was a chilly winter's evening, and I was sitting on the floor sorting out some papers, when suddenly, there was a loud but distant explosion, which shook the house and vibrated through the floorboards. It had come from the east Greenwich area, and I rushed to a nearby balcony, where I looked north towards the river to see a chaotic scene. A large gasometer had been bombed and was on fire, with tongues of red, blue, and yellow flames leaping out violently, thirty metres above the crumpled shell. Several fire engines had already arrived, and as I watched it seemed that flashing blue lights of the emergency services were speeding towards Greenwich from every corner of London.

This gasometer was one of several close together and there was a real danger of more exploding. This part of London was a run-down industrial area at the time, but there were a few residents living nearby who were being hastily evacuated from the scene. This attack would have brought back stark memories to many of the older residents, who had lived through the dreadful days of the blitz and rocket attacks in World War II, when thousands died. Luckily, the remaining gasometers did not explode, but the blue lights continued flashing well into the night. It was a reminder to be constantly vigilant as we travelled around London during those troubled and unsettling times.

Irish workers living in London kept a low profile to avoid abuse, and Provisional IRA sympathisers targeted them in the pubs of north and west London to raise money. They were often threatened if they did not donate. It was a difficult time for many of them, who just wanted to work and earn some money for their families back home.

On May 5 1981 Bobby Sands, aged 27, an IRA leader serving a long prison sentence in the Maze prison in Northern Ireland, died after a sixty-six-day hunger strike. The unions on the barrier requested that the site close for a day, which was agreed after a board meeting debate. There were rumours going around that the IRA had a sleeper cell on the barrier, waiting to plant a bomb in one of the sills.

Thankfully, it was nothing but rumour, and no illegal explosives were ever found on the site, but it was a nervous time for us all, nonetheless.

10

1982 – 84

1982

After the excellent progress made in the last twelve months, the civil works team could at last see the finish line. There was still much to do on the north side, removing the temporary works and making sure DCBC had access to install the final gate at span G, and to complete the dredging and bed protection works. This was required for Key Date 6, and was achieved by the beginning of April.

DOWNRIVER FLOOD PROTECTION

The Thames Barrier was only part of the wider plan to prevent flooding in the Thames estuary. Defence work was necessary downriver of the barrier as well, and this work had to be completed at the same time as the construction of the barrier. It was also imperative the work wasn't finished before the barrier. If a surge wave came, it would be funnelled upriver by the new embankments, and with the barrier incomplete, London would then be extremely vulnerable to flooding.

A huge amount of work was required, with the banks and

flood walls along 112 kilometres of shoreline needing to be raised. Four separate authorities were involved - the GLC, Southern Water, Thames Water and Anglian Water. The work included the building of a further five smaller barriers. The largest was the Barking Barrier across the River Roding at Barking Creek to protect the huge Beckton sewage treatment works, the Dartford Barrier that goes across the Dartford Creek, and the Fobbing Horse and Easthaven barriers, which are part of the Canvey Island protection works. Two substantial flood gates were also required for the main entrance to the Royal and Tilbury docks, which each weighed 200 tonnes.

There is little standardisation in the design of the flood defences, and construction of banks in tidal estuaries can be extremely difficult. The weather is frequently inclement, the ground conditions are soft and variable, which change with surge tides, making plant and personnel access difficult.

The first contract was let in 1974, and sixty-eight more contracts followed, lasting into the early eighties. They included a wide variety of schemes, from dredging works, to driving many kilometres of sheet piling, requiring concrete cappings. Many simple earth banks needed to be built, and thousands of tonnes of rock protection needed to be installed along the shoreline. This would all come in at a total cost of 300 million pounds.

There were 1500 operatives working on these projects, supervised by 375 consulting engineers and 200 staff from the various authorities, so it involved a lot of complex coordination between all the parties. For the majority of this work to be completed by 1983 was an amazing achievement by all the engineers and administrators involved.

RIVER BED PROTECTION

In June 1971, in the early days of the design, the barrier consultants, RPT, had awarded a contract to the Hydraulic Research Station (HRS) at Wallingford, in Oxfordshire, to carry out a study to determine the effects of the velocity of the river in Woolwich Reach, as a result of the construction of the barrier. A 1:300 model of Woolwich Reach was built in concrete, with a vertical scale of 1:60 in the HRS shed at Wallingford. Tests were started in November to investigate the changes of river velocity due to the position of the cofferdams during construction, and the final alignment of the piers.

In addition, they also carried out a study to check what dredging and river bed protection was required, using a further two models. These determined the effect of normal closure of the gates with undershot flow, and the effect of the failure of one gate to close. This showed where the worst scour would occur, and the areas where bed protection would be required. From these results, RPT drew up the design, and that scope of work became part of the CTHJV contract.

CTHJV awarded a sub-contract to marine specialists HAM-ACZ Thames Consortium (Anglo-Dutch) to undertake this work. This covered the dredging of the river bed for the sill sinking, preparation of the river bed for the bed protection, and placing prefabricated mattresses, which had to be floated into position before being lowered onto the river bed. Finally, placing and profiling 250,000 tonnes of filter stone and armour rock on the mattresses to seal the bed protection. Further sea-dredged gravel was also placed at the edge of the mattresses to prevent further scour. This involved extensive dredging in the centre of the river, both upriver and downriver of the barrier, which was carried out by an impressive, barge-mounted digger nicknamed Popeye by the marine team, which was capable of excavating to a depth of 30 metres. A flotilla of barges was required to deliver the rock, ranging in size from 400 kilograms to six tonnes, with the larger rocks individually placed by barge-mounted cranes under the supervision of marine engineers. One of those was CTHJV section engineer Ken Limburn, from Portsmouth, who worked on the barrier for over three years. With the constant arrival and manoeuvring of waterborne craft, it was a busy time for the ever-watchful watermen.

COMPLETION OF THE GATES

After the success of the installation of the gate in span C, the remaining gate arms and gate leaves were all installed in a frenetic twelve weeks. Span G, between Piers 3 and 4, was the final lift and completed in April.

Dick Thorp was delighted and gave all the credit to his excellent team from Darlington. It had been going so well they were able to reduce the working hours from 24 hours a day to 40 hours a week, with no loss in production, despite being dictated to by the tides for the heavy lifts.

Meanwhile, the mechanical and electrical works, and installation of the control systems were following close behind. These teams got all the machinery installed, bolted up, and connected. Hundreds of miles of cabling had to be threaded down through the piers into the service tunnels, terminating in the control rooms.

HANDOVER

John Grice had now achieved all his goals, garnering praise from the client, the consultant and his staff, and he returned to Costain's Head Office to become Chairman of Costain Civil Engineering and Construction.

Adrian Franklin took over as Project Manager and Warren Hibbs became Deputy Project Manager to complete the pier works, remove all the temporary works and access jetties and complete the bedding protection works. This achieved the final Key Date 7 on August 13.

There was only very limited industrial action once the Supplemental Agreement was introduced, and that would not have been possible without the major contribution that the convenor steward, Bruce Birdsell, and his team made during this period, quickly settling any disagreements that arose on site.

CONTROL ROOMS

Often overlooked are the two building complexes at either end of the barrier. These are the nerve centres for the control, operation, power supply, maintenance and administration of the barrier. The south side is dominated by an impressive, 60m-high control building, with a striking, elliptically shaped, concave roof, clad with stainless-steel. On the seventh floor, there is a large observation window, with a panoramic view of the north side, as well as clear views upriver and downriver.

This work was not carried out by CTHJV, but had been awarded to Sindall Construction of Cambridge for £5,500,000 pounds. The contract also included a generator house, work-shops, sub-stations, an underground car park, service subways, operating decks and ramps, public walkways, a gatehouse and boundary walls. On the north side there were sub-stations, service subways, a gatehouse and boundary walls. As the civil works came to an end, the areas were gradually handed over to Sindalls to start their building works, vital for completion.

FIRST CLOSURE October 31

In the early hours of the morning on Sunday October 31, out of the glare of the media, a large number of engineers gathered at strategic points along the barrier to observe every major component, for the closing of all ten of the gates together for the first time. There was confidence in the air, but inevitable tension, as the button was pressed in the control room by the leader of the testing team.

It was overseen by the new barrier manager, John Hounslow, who had been a senior civil engineer with the RPT site team for ten years, and knew every detail of the barrier.

Fifteen minutes after pressing the button, the rising sector gates emerged glistening out of the water in conjunction with the falling radial gates, and moved smoothly to the closure position. It was a complete success, and greeted with much applause and relief.

The barrier had now proven to be operational if a surge tide occurred, and central London could at last be fully protected.

MORE TESTING

The first test closure of the barrier was made at low water, for a period of less than three hours. The structure now needed to be tested by closing the gates with the tide flooding at maximum velocity. This was carried out the following Sunday, with the gates being closed at half-flood tide, and opened when the tide was at half-ebb.

During this period, the maximum level difference across the gates built up to four metres. This produced a load of over 2,600 tonnes on each of the central 61m-wide gates, and was carried with no apparent effect. Analysis of the measurements of the gate deflections showed these to be as predicted.

Meanwhile there were many minor works to be carried out for completion.

Some permanent cabling and switch gear still had to be installed, where temporary equipment had been used for the testing, and a variety of remedial works went on for months, but none of these works stopped the barrier from operating.

The official opening date of the barrier was still to be announced, waiting for essential parts of the downriver flood protection works to be completed.

INTERNATIONAL DISTRACTIONS

Although the barrier's completion was greeted with great relief in Whitehall, it was rather overshadowed by international events that had occurred earlier in the year.

On April 2 1982, Argentina had invaded the Falkland Islands, a small, British-owned archipelago in the South Atlantic, and claimed them as Argentinian territory. They renamed them Las Malvinas. This triggered an undeclared war with the United Kingdom lasting seventy-four days, and was an enormous test for Margaret Thatcher and her ailing government. She decided to send troops to fight a war 8,000 miles away on the other side of the world.

The first landings took place on April 24 on South Georgia and after a brief skirmish with the small garrison, the island was swiftly retaken. A naval task force arrived in May and an amphibious assault was launched. After several hard-fought battles, and many casualties on both sides, the capital, Stanley, was taken back on June 14, with an Argentinian surrender.

The troops were greeted as heroes on their return to Portsmouth, and it was considered a great victory. It lifted the morale of the country and saved Margaret Thatcher. Despite a recession, she went on to win the next election decisively, held on June 9 1983.

The country was gripped by this distant war, so little attention was paid to the progress on the barrier.

1982 CONCRETE SOCIETY AWARD

The design was starting to garner awards. In 1982, The Concrete Society awarded its civil engineering category to the Thames Barrier. The judges commented:

'This whole flood protection scheme is a milestone in civil engineering. In particular, attention is drawn to the deep-profiled precast sill units which link with the mechanical components, and demonstrate a superb example of concrete engineering.'

1983
THE FIRST SURGE

The new team in the control room did not have to wait long for the barrier's first real test.

On February 1, 1983, a surge wave came down the east coast, symbolically, exactly thirty years after the disastrous 1953 flood.

The warning system worked smoothly. The tide gauges had been installed down the east coast with telemetry links, and sent back the water level data to the Tyne, (there is also a smaller barrier at Immingham), and Southend meteorological stations, which sent the data and an alert to the barrier control centre.

A new VAX 11/750 computer had been installed, (costing £500,000), which quickly calculated the final predicted water levels from the input tide, river flow and weather information for central London. The button was pressed for the gates to be raised.

The whole operation went like clockwork, and this vital test proved the barrier was ready.

Media attention increased and on May 25, 1983 a stamp was issued by the Royal Post as part of the celebrations for British engineering achievements.

1984
THE OPENING, May 8

There had been much debate and lobbying on the kind of opening the barrier should be given. Many thought it should be a Royal opening, but the GLC, which had a Labour majority led by pro-Republican leader, Ken Livingstone, was against it.

He changed his mind when he was allowed to accompany Her Majesty and Prince Philip on the royal barge from Westminster with his mother.

Harvey Linds, the Chairman of the GLC wrote,

'The barrier was built and designed to keep Londoners safe from any possible surge-tide flooding, and is undoubtedly one of the greatest engineering feats of the century, and is something of which the (Greater London) Council is very proud. Because the barrier is unique – there is nothing like it anywhere else in the world, the designers, engineers and workforce were breaking new ground, and using techniques to enable Londoners to live in safety… The Queen's presence will be a fitting recognition of a magnificent accomplishment.'

John Reeve wrote as Chairman of Costain Civil Engineering and CTHJV, 'We feel that this major project is a credit to British engineering and to the British construction industry, and deserves the worldwide publicity with a Royal opening.'

The requests were listened to, and after discussions with HM The Queen, it was agreed to open the Thames Barrier on Tuesday May 8 1984.

The celebration was to be given massive publicity, and televised worldwide. It was a fitting tribute to the employees of many companies from all over Britain and worldwide who had worked so hard in getting the barrier completed before disaster could strike.

On May 8, on a grey and very chilly afternoon, Queen Elizabeth II and the Duke of Edinburgh stepped aboard the Royal barge named the *Royal Nore* at Festival Pier, adjacent to the South

Bank Arts complex in Waterloo. It was a twin-screw motor ship originally owned by the Port of London Authority, and had been operating as the Royal barge since 1971. The Royal Standard and regalia were displayed, and Her Majesty was accompanied by her Royal Bargemaster, Edwin Hunt MVO, along with eight Royal Watermen, in full ceremonial dress standing on the fore-deck.

They set off to Woolwich Reach with massive security measures en route. Additional police had been drafted in, divers searched under all the bridges, commercial ships on the Thames were stopped, and helicopters banned from flying overhead. *The Royal Nore* set off on the fifty-minute journey at a regal pace, passing bunting-strewn offices, bridges and wharfs, with large crowds cheering enthusiastically, despite the cold and occasional rain.

They entered Woolwich Reach fifty minutes later, to be greeted by a flotilla of small boats and a cacophony of klaxons and ship's hooters. Unfortunately, these also drowned out the gentle sounds of Handel's *Water Music* being played by the Newham Borough Band.

I was on one of the boats with a group of staff from Costain, (I was now working with Costain International based in London, and had just returned from the Middle East), and watched the Royal barge glide regally by, only twenty metres away. The liveried watermen were standing to attention, with four either side of the fore-deck, and the Royal Bargemaster, (who started life as a waterman) standing proudly at the bow. They looked splendid in their skirted, scarlet tunics with a silver-gilt royal cypher on the front and back of the jacket, breeches, a navy/black cap, scarlet stockings, white shirt and black, buckled shoes. It was British pageantry at its best.

At 15:30, Her Majesty alighted at the Barrier Garden Pier to be greeted by Baroness Philipps, Lord Lieutenant of the City of London. She introduced the Queen and Prince Philip to the Rt. Hon. Lord Jopling, who at that time was the Minister of Agriculture, Harvey Hinds, the Chairman of the GLC, and Ken Livingstone, the leader of the GLC, who was reluctant to attend, but looked as though he was quietly enjoying the occasion.

Temporary stands had been erected, where hundreds of dignitaries, guests, barrier staff and workers, and local families were gathered, waving flags furiously trying to keep warm, with the ladies desperately hanging on to their hats.

Alistair Handford was sitting in the stands next to a regal-looking wife of a senior member of the GLC, who had really gone to town on her face make-up. After an hour in the Siberian winds she turned to say something, and to Alistair's horror and fascination, he found himself looking at a face, shot-blasted to the foundation, but only on the side exposed to the bitter wind.

The Queen stood on a podium with Prince Philip and made a short speech, praising the barrier and those who had worked so hard building it, and added that

'...it had indeed been a race against the tide, and could be described as one of the engineering wonders of the world.'

With that royal seal of approval, the console button was pressed to signal the gates to be set in motion for the official closure. It was greeted with great applause and another crescendo of klaxons. Fifteen minutes later, the massive gates started to appear above the waves to more cheers, klaxons, and fountains of water from the fire-boats. The gates rose slowly and smoothly to their closed position, forming a thin, black line across the mighty Thames, guarded by their silver-hooded sentinels, the row of nine majestic piers with the stainless-steel roofs shimmering in the distance.

Lines of dignitaries waited to be introduced to The Queen and the Duke of Edinburgh, who was greatly enjoying the occasion. They included Ray Horner from the GLC, who had seen the project through from its conception. Peter Cox, Chairman of Rendel Palmer and Tritton, introduced the RPT team, starting with George Davies, the engineer's representative on site from beginning to end, and representatives from the design teams, including Alan Mitchell, the chief design manager of all the civils works, and Dick Tappin, the chief design manager of the gates.

Representatives from the contractors were next, led by John Reeve, Chairman of Costain Engineering and the CTHJV, who introduced John Grice, the Project Manager, Terrel Wyatt, the Group Chairman of Costain, Mr. E Pountain, the Chairman of Tarmac Construction, and Mr. C Molenaar, from Holland, the parent board representative of HBG, (the parent company of HBM). Davy-Cleveland Barrier Consortium was represented by Bill Maisey, the Project Director and Dick Thorp, the Project Manager, and a long line of others followed, including representatives from Sindalls of Cambridge, Tysons Ltd. of Liverpool, and many others around Britain who had played an important part in bringing the Thames Barrier to reality.

The Queen and Duke of Edinburgh were then shown round the control tower and introduced to John Hounslow, the new barrier captain, who introduced the team now running and maintaining the barrier.

Hundreds of excited local children were given the day off from school to join in the celebrations, and left with unforgettable memories. When the royal launch finally departed from Barrier Garden Pier later that afternoon, it left a day of spectacular memories of this unique occasion, and a wonderful celebration of one of the wonders of the modern world.

I was sent this poem by Bill Reynolds. It is called _The Wonderful Eighth_ by Lester McGonagall. This is the abridged version.

By the double Woolwich Ferry
Near the tunnel they call Blackwall,
From the north bank to the south bank
Stretch the Piers and Rolling Gates.
Holding back at the press of a button
Waters which, when their highest
Threaten flooding of the City.

... Now the chosen tide and chosen day,
Down the river sailed the convoy.
Three o'clock on the eighth of May
Carrying the Queen of England
To the Eighth of Modern Wonders,
Doing what Canute could not.

Thousands waited for the moment.
All the multitudes were waiting.
Cold the day but warm the welcome.

London was no more in danger
From the menaces of Nature's
Strongest winds and highest tides.
So, She closed the massive gateways
And declared the barrier open.

EPILOGUE

In 2024, the Thames Barrier will have been in operation for 40 years, and has never let us down. It has been tested many times, and prevented London from catastrophic flooding. Those living and working in London can take comfort that as they move around, their homes, businesses, utilities and underground stations are all safe from inundation.

Until November 2023, the gates have been raised 209 times, far more than was originally intended. Not only has it been used 118 times to protect against surge tides and flooding, but also 91 times for fluvial flooding. This is where the barrier is used when there is very heavy rain to the west of London. It can delay the Thames from rising too quickly by creating an overspill reservoir, preventing, in the worst case, the river possibly spilling over the embankments in central London.

Due to the effects of increased global warming, this is going to happen more often.

The barrier was also raised for sixteen hours on August 20, 1989 to delay the incoming tide, helping with the recovery of a sunken pleasure boat, the *Marchioness,* after a tragic collision near Southwark Bridge. The boat was carrying 130 people for a birthday celebration, and was in collision with the dredger *Bowbelle.* Tragically, fifty-one people died that night, with an average age of twenty-two.

Marine craft have been involved in fifteen collisions with the barrier, the most serious in the early morning of October 27, 1997, when a 98m-long dredger called the *Sand Kite*, laden with 3,300 tonnes of aggregate, struck Pier 5 in dense fog.

The ship was holed and started taking on water immediately. It tried to move astern, but at this point it had taken on too much water and sank. It came to rest on the river bed, on top of the barrier gate, spilling the majority of the aggregate in the process. The thirteen crew were rescued, and luckily, none hurt, apart from the Captain's pride.

This was one of the worst scenarios the barrier team had envisaged. The ship was stuck fast and the barrier could not be fully closed, leaving London vulnerable if a storm surge occurred.

Urgent emergency procedures were immediately implemented, with a salvage team arriving the following day. It took five days to release the stricken craft and remove the thousands of tonnes of aggregate on the gate. There was minor damage to the pier concrete, but there was more serious damage to the corrosion protection on the gate, caused by abrasion of the aggregate.

On November 9 2007, the barrier was closed due to a surge tide as strong as the disastrous 1953 surge. It raced down the east coast, but fortunately on this occasion, did not coincide with the London high tide.

With global warming causing increasingly more powerful storms each year, the risk of catastrophic floods occurring in this country are escalating. In 2013, the gates were raised fifty times in an exceptional year for storms.

The 1973 surge predictions for 2030 have already been exceeded, and planning is underway to identify the location for the next barrier. Information about the Thames Barrier from the original studies in the 1950s and 60s is still available, and relevant, and is providing invaluable knowledge towards the design of its successor.

The location will need to be further downriver, towards the Isle of Sheppey, where the Thames is wider. It will take longer to build, and consequently, will be substantially more expensive. No doubt this will inevitably create delays in persuading future politicians to approve the funds.

When the second barrier is built, the United Kingdom will be a very different country compared to 1974. Our universities will still be producing highly talented civil engineers who will want to work on the design and construction of inspiring civil engineering projects such as this. However, the sourcing of materials and the fabricators will be very different. The rush to globalisation in the 1980s has decimated our manufacturing capability. Few of the companies that worked on the barrier in the 1970s still exist. (Cleveland Bridge sadly closed in Darlington in 2021).

It is considered far cheaper to fabricate in the Far East. This is fine in times of peace and prosperity, but will put us in a very vulnerable position if international relations deteriorate. Regrettably, UK manufacturers will be incapable of supplying most of the materials to build the next Thames Barrier.

An international consortium will probably construct it, with one of our major contractors taking the lead. Our contractors are now dominated by a handful of large, multinational companies capable of delivering every type of infrastructure.

Costain are a good example, forming consortiums for the largest projects and employing large sub-contractors to carry out the work. That trend looks likely to continue.

It is probable there will be a shortage of skilled workers, despite big advances in AI equipment. Much of the work will doubtless be carried out by fewer, highly skilled technicians, and some very clever machines.

There is also a possibility the existing barrier will be given a new life after it is decommissioned. With the strong and increasing demand for green energy, one idea is to convert the barrier into a mini hydro-electric dam, installing turbines in the outer channels, or even water wheels, and keep the larger, central channels open for shipping. Another suggestion is using the piers as supports for a small pedestrian and cycling bridge across the Thames.

Meanwhile, the Environmental Agency (EA), the operators of the barrier since 1996, have found ways to increase the height of the gates a little, to stay ahead of the surges, which may hold until 2070, if we are lucky. There will also be a requirement for the downriver embankments to be increased in height in the near future, because of the rising waters.

A small exhibition centre was built at the barrier, run by the EA, and has been very popular with school parties and with tourists. It was incredibly disappointing to discover that many of the visiting schoolchildren were completely unaware that the Thames Barrier existed. They had no idea that one of the wonders of the modern world was right on their doorstep.

On October 31 1992, there was a reunion at the barrier, when over eighty personnel from RPT and CTHJV gathered to celebrate ten years since the barrier started operating. These included six from HBM, who had flown across from the Netherlands. Ray Horner, (by then retired) came to the barrier especially to welcome us, and was beaming like a proud father. There were only a few that had worked from start to finish on the construction of the barrier, and even fewer that had been in the control room, so for many of us, there was the pleasure of learning new things about the barrier that day.

Many wives and partners also attended, who could now understand, and see for themselves the scale of the project and what we had achieved. The day concluded with a fine dinner in a new hotel in Surrey docks, which has been transformed from the derelict area we remember in the 1970s. Luxury flats, new office blocks, and rail links have now been built, signalling a promising future being created in that part of London.

Many of those who visited in 1992 are now no longer with us, but of the remainder that have contributed to the book over the past year, they clearly have good memories of the people they worked with, and enormous pride in having been involved in the construction of the truly iconic Thames Barrier.

ACKNOWLEDGEMENTS

When I first started my research for this book, I was concerned about how many of us that worked on the Thames Barrier would still be around. I did not need to worry, the answer was, many. They came forward from all over the UK with many stories, and found boxes stowed away in their lofts containing all sorts of treasures.

So, many thanks to the CTHJV managers and engineers who worked with me on the barrier, including Adrian Franklin, Bob Napthine, Warren Hibbs, Paul Sivey, Rick Randall, Peter Blaseby, Mike Burnett, John Key, and especially Alistair Handford, who rescued a lot of the copies of *Costain News* from the archives before they were destroyed. Also, special thanks to Phil Grice, the son of John Grice, who showed me his father's unique memorabilia. Also to Sam Cornberg, with whom I had worked on Pier 9, and is still living in Greenwich, for a nostalgic visit to the barrier after many years.

Thanks also to Bill Reynolds, who worked for RPT in 1976, and who I met up with again when we worked in Hong Kong. He put me in touch with Dick Thorp of DCBC, and John Welch, one of the senior steel inspectors at RPT. He was able to supply old copies of the *Rendel News* and details of the fabrication yard that no longer exists. He also introduced me to Alan Mitchell, who had started to work on the design of the barrier with RPT in 1972 as their Chief Engineer for the Civil

Works, and who worked with and knew Charlie Draper well.

Also thanks to the staff at the ICE library for digging through their archives, and to Richard Bayfield for his help with the ICE.

Finally, thanks again to my editors Russell Kilmister and Fiona Ritchie for their speed and patience, to Terry Bannon for the great cover design, and being able to make sense of my photos, to Charlotte Mourncey for her fine typesetting, and to my publisher James Essinger of Conrad Press for his advice and assistance.

THAMES BARRIER FACTS

Width of the River Thames at the barrier	= 520m
Width between the barrier abutments	= 560m
Total No of Piers	= 9
Total No of Abutments	= 2
Length of Longest Piers (4-8)	= 65m
Width of Widest Piers (4-8)	= 11m
Level of deepest pier foundation (Pier 4)	= -24m

CONCRETE

Largest Underwater Concrete Pour (Pier 4)	= 6,600m³
Volume in Piers	= 168,000m³
Volume in Sills	= 33,000 m³
Volume in Abutments	= 13,000m³
Total	= 214,000m³

STEEL

Total No of Gates	= 10
No of 61m span Rising Sector Gates (RSG)	= 4
No of 31.5m span RSG	= 2
No of 31.5m span Falling Radial Gates (FRG)	= 4
Weight of a 61m RSG	= 3,200t
Weight of a 31.5 m RSG	= 900t
Weight of a 31.5m FRG	= 200t
Steel in all gates and supports	= 36,000t
Reinforcement	= 10,000t
Machinery	= 5,000t
Total	= 51,000t

(t= tonnes)

GLOSSARY OF ABBREVIATIONS

AI	Artificial Intelligence
ASBSBSW	Amalgamated Society of Boilermakers, Shipwrights, Blacksmiths and Structural Workers
CAD	Computer Aided Design
CBE	Commander of the Order of the British Empire
CTHJV	Costain Civil Engineering, Tarmac Construction, Hollandsche Beton Maatschappij Joint Venture
DCBC	Davy-Loewy Cleveland Bridge Consortium
EA	Environmental Agency
FICE	Fellow of the Institution of Engineers
GLC	Greater London Council
GPS	Global Positioning System
HBG	Hollandsche Beton Group (Parent of HBM)
HBM	Hollandsche Beton Maatschappij BV
HRS	Hydraulic Research Station
ICE	Institution of Civil Engineers
LCC	London County Council
MAFF	Ministry of Agriculture, Fisheries and Food

MBE	Member of the Order of the British Empire
MICE	Member of the Institution of Civil Engineers
PLA	Port of London Authority
RPT	Rendel, Palmer and Tritton
TGWU	Transport and General Workers' Union
TML	Transmarche Link
UCATT	Union of Construction, Allied Trades and Technicians

BIBLIOGRAPHY

Books referred in Text

ANGLO-SAXON CHRONICLES Anon., Anne Savage, Heinemann, London

GILBERT S., HORNER R., 1984, *THE THAMES BARRIER,* Thomas Telford Ltd.

PATTEN C., 2022, *THE HONG KONG DIARIES*, Allen Lane Publishing

WILSON K., 1989 *THE STORY OF THE THAMES BARRIER,* 1989, Lanthorn Publishing

Newspapers and magazines referred to in Text

CONTRACT JOURNAL SUPPLEMENT May 1984, *THAMES BARRIER, A Salute to Achievement*

CONSTRUCTION NEWS SUPPLEMENT Nov 1982, *THAMES BARRIER, A Review of the Thames Flood Defences*

COSTAIN NEWS, the Costain Group International Newspaper *Various editions 1977-1982*

THE CTHJV THAMES BARRIER PROGRESS MAGAZINE *Various editions 1977- 1982*

THE LONDONER, newspaper April 1984, Greater London Council

NEW CIVIL ENGINEER SUPPLEMENT 1982, *THE THAMES BARRIER*, Thomas Telford Ltd.

NEW CIVIL ENGINEER MAGAZINE Sept 1977, Thomas Telford Ltd.

NEW CIVIL ENGINEER MAGAZINE July 1980 *Progress at a Price,* Thomas Telford Ltd.

NEW CIVIL ENGINEER MAGAZINE Nov 1982. Thomas Telford Ltd.
NEW CIVIL ENGINEER MAGAZINE May 1984 *Barrier Royal,* Thomas Telford Ltd.
NEW CIVIL ENGINEER MAGAZINE May 2009 *Jewel of the Thames,* Thomas Telford Ltd.

Papers and Articles referred to in Text

BONDI, H. 1967 *LONDON FLOOD BARRIER, Report to Ministry of Housing and Local Government*

THAMES BARRAGE COMMITTEE, 1907, *THE PORT OF LONDON AND THE THAMES BARRAGE*

GLC 1968, *THAMES BARRIER, THAMES FLOOD PREVENTION,* 1st Report

GLC 1971, *THAMES BARRIER, THAMES FLOOD PREVENTION,* 2nd Report

GRICE J. R, and HEPPLEWHITE E. A., 1983, *DESIGN AND CONSTRUCTION OF THE THAMES BARRIER COFFERDAMS,* ICE Paper 8629, ICE Part 1

GRICE J. R. and BLASEBY P., 1983, *MECHANICAL PLANT TECHNIQUES EMPLOYED ON THE THAMES BARRIER DURING THE CIVIL ENGINEERING WORKS CONTRACT,* INSTITUTION of MECHANICAL ENGINEERS - Paper presented 8 June 1983

Other references in Text

COSTAIN GROUP FILM UNIT, 1984 – *TAMING THE THAMES*
ENVIRONMENT AGENCY 2014 – *THE THAMES BARRIER*
GLC 1984 – Public Relations Publicity Photographs
RENDELL PALMER AND TRITTON, Poem – *The Wonderful Eighth*
STOUGHTON, Patricia, - Online stories *Ebb and Flow on the Tidal Thames*
THAMES TELEVISION 1984 – Coverage of the Opening of the Thames Barrier

INDEX

I

J

R

S

ABOUT THE AUTHOR

Rory O'Grady has been writing books for over fifteen years, specialising in biographies and non-fiction. *We Gave a Dam* is his fourth. Rory has travelled extensively, working in civil engineering management in the UK, Nigeria and Saudi Arabia, and spent twenty years in Hong Kong.

The five years he spent working on the Thames Barrier as a young civil engineer were life changing, and inspirational. *We Gave a Dam* is a tribute to the numerous engineers, managers and workers he was lucky enough to work with, and to the many he never met.

Rory retired to Canterbury, in Kent in South East England, and continues writing.